D1267913

Jesus in the Gospel of Matthew

EDWARD P. BLAIR

JESUS IN THE GOSPEL OF MATTHEW

ABINGDON PRESS NEW YORK • NASHVILLE

JESUS IN THE GOSPEL OF MATTHEW

Library of Congress Catalog Card Number: 60-12067

SET UP, PRINTED, AND BOUND BY THE PARTHENON PRESS, AT NASHVILLE, TENNESSEE, UNITED STATES OF AMERICA

To my students—
present and former—
in gratitude for their
friendship,
inspiration,
and forbearance

PREFACE

THE Gospels are both intriguing and baffling books. Like snowcapped mountain peaks shimmering above the desert heat, they beckon the traveler on, only to slow his ascent by offering massive scarp and deadly crevasses to his stumbling feet. But the climb is exhilarating precisely because it is difficult, and the moments of vision and understanding seem to turn the scarp into a staircase.

The Gospel of Matthew has been particularly stubborn in yielding up its secrets. No sure conclusions have been reached by scholars concerning its authorship, date, place of writing, original readers, purpose, and general theological point of view. Its place at the head of the canon symbolizes the regard in which it was held by the ancient church; and the widespread familiarity today with the Sermon on the Mount shows that its glories are not wholly unappreciated by twentieth-century men. But the average contemporary reader is painfully aware that he stands only in the foothills.

This book is an attempt to scale a few of the lower eminences. I first undertook the venture some twenty years ago with a doctoral dissertation in the field of Matthean Christology, which was accepted by the faculty of Yale University Divinity School. The many questions which could not be answered at that stage of New Testament research led me to abandon the investigation for a while. But the urge returned to take up the project again, this time with the better equipment made available by the advance of New Testament scholarship. Of particular significance is the new understanding of the Jewish background of Christianity which has resulted from discovery of the Qumran texts (the Dead Sea Scrolls).

It is not the purpose of these studies to examine carefully the perplexing historical questions connected with the origin of the Gospel of Matthew. My objective is rather to identify and characterize the distinctive elements in the author's Christology. What exactly is Matthew's Jesus like? A definition and characterization of this sort is to some extent possible without final answers to the historical questions. But only "to some extent." When one begins to point out the relevance of this Christology for the church of Matthew's time and to assess its place in the pattern of New Testament Christology as a whole, one comes hard against the thorny historical problems. I have made no attempt to evade the historical questions, as Chapter I and parts of Chapter V will show, but it is not the focus of my interest.

At the very beginning it should be stated that the name "Matthew" is used in this book as a convenient designation of the author of the First Gospel, whoever he may have been. It is hardly likely that the apostle Matthew was the writer of the Gospel in its present form. It is possible, however, that he was connected somehow with materials utilized in it. Occasionally "Matthew" stands in this book for the Gospel. The context will indicate whether the person or the book is meant.

Chapter I, a survey of recent scholarly discussions of several of the important historical problems, may seem in the light of what has just been said about the objective of these studies to be somewhat irrelevant. But the survey will serve as background to the examination of the Christology in Chapters II-IV and offer the reader a convenient summary of what is being said concerning basic questions. In Chapter V an epitome of Matthew's Christology is presented, a tentative suggestion concerning the affinities of Matthew's thought is hazarded, and a few remarks are made about the meaning of the portrait of Jesus in the Gospel of Matthew for the times in which it first appeared.

I regard the chief contribution of the studies here presented to be a more adequate characterization (as it appears to me) of Matthew's view of the way of salvation. Salvation, for him, results from understanding the mysteries of God's redemptive purposes and activities as mediated through Jesus, the Son; from faith in and loyalty to Jesus as eschatological Deliverer; from inner righteousness and loving attitudes; from merciful deeds as an expression of a benevolent spirit. Matthew's thought on this subject thus revolves around four centers: understanding, believing, being, and doing. The words of Jesus, together with his deeds, constitute a revelation from the Father by which the disciple is led to the response suggested in these four words. When one makes this kind of a response to God's revelation in Jesus, he fulfills the will of God as expressed in the Old Testament. The Gospel of Matthew is a "Gospel," not simply a code of conduct (a new *Halakah*), a handbook of church administration, or a manual of worship.

The longer I study Matthew's Christology the more similarities I find to the Christology of the Fourth Gospel. It is suggested in the last chapter (for the first time, so far as I am aware) that the writers of these two Gospels came out of the same circle of early Christian thought, namely, that represented by the Hellenists of Jerusalem, of whom Stephen was an important leader. It has been proposed recently that the Fourth Evangelist was connected with this circle. It is not argued here that the writer of the Gospel of Matthew had himself been a member of the Jerusalem community—though I think this is not impossible—but only that he was in touch with the kind of thought represented in Stephen's last address (Acts 7). Whether such a position will prove to be sound remains to be seen. It is hoped that this tentative suggestion will not blind the reader to the central objective of these studies —characterization of Matthew's Christology, rather than explanations of it.

Unfortunately, the important book by Günther Bornkamm, Gerhard Barth, and Heinz Joachim Held, *Überlieferung und Auslegung im Matthäusevangelium* (Neukirchen Kreis Moers, 1960) was published after my manuscript had reached the galley stage. Only occasional references to it appear therefore in the footnotes. However, the misfortune is somewhat mitigated by the fact that Professor Bornkamm's contributions to the book had been published previously and Gerhard Barth's research in the form of a doctoral dissertation was available to me in the library of the University of Heidelberg in the summer of 1956. With many of the views of Bornkamm and his students I find myself in agreement. Some points of difference will appear in the discussion to follow.

I wish to express my gratitude to Millar Burrows, for many years Winkley Professor of Biblical Theology at Yale University, under whose direction the research on Matthew was begun. He is, of course, in no way responsible for the views expressed here these many years later. A student of a distinquished professor can only wish that his efforts were more of a credit to his learned mentor.

Thanks also are due Hans Rudolf Merkel of Basel, Switzerland, a house guest of several months, who assisted me in various ways during the writing of this book, several Garrett students who offered helpful criticisms of the manuscript in a seminar on Matthew's Christology, and my wife for the typing of the manuscript.

EDWARD P. BLAIR

CONTENTS

[1]

Major Issues in Matthean Studies

THE Gospels cast a peculiar spell over those who read them thoughtfully and repeatedly. The French orientalist and littérateur of the last century, Ernest Renan, felt this spell and rhapsodized over these "masterpieces of spontaneous art," as he regarded them, "in which every defect is a beauty" and which have power, as have no other writings, to "conquer hearts." [1] Though he praised the literary qualities of these writings, he recognized that their true power lies in the grandeur of the person they present. In a real sense, said he, "Jesus was . . . the author of his own biography." [2]

There can be little doubt that Renan is right in affirming that it is Jesus himself who has given the Gospels their power. But it is hardly correct to regard them as biographies. The Gospels are quite different in literary form from Suetonius' *Lives of the Caesars* or Plutarch's *Parallel Lives*. The Gospels show little interest in subjects which are the stock in trade of the biographer, ancient or modern: family background (social status, achievements, vocation), education, physical and

[1] *Les Évangiles et la seconde génération chrétienne* (Paris, 1877), pp. 99-100.
[2] *Ibid.*, p. 101.

mental qualities, personal habits, domestic and public experiences in chronological sequence, and the like.

Neither are the Gospels memoirs, like Xenophon's *Memorabilia,* in spite of the fact that the apologist Justin of the second century so described them. In memoir literature the writer's personality is invariably prominent. However, in the Gospels, as A. E. J. Rawlinson has said, the writers disappear behind their materials.[3] Their books are anonymous; they want the reader to see Jesus only.

And the Jesus they disclose is not the Jesus seen by one man or by four men but in a real sense by the whole church. The Form Historians were partly right in de-emphasizing the role of the evangelists in the creation of the Gospels and in highlighting the contribution of the primitive Christian community as a whole. The Gospels have resulted from the crystallization of the church's memories of Jesus. These recollections were put together by individuals and to a degree interpreted by them. But the resultant Gospels are hardly their original creations. Luke freely confesses his indebtedness to the many narratives that lay at hand and to the eyewitnesses behind them (Luke 1:1-4). He wanted it known that he was no novelist or innovator but only a faithful recorder of the church's recollections of Jesus.

The precise extent to which individuals, on the one hand, and the Christian community, on the other, are responsible for the creation of the Gospels is perhaps indeterminable. But that the Gospels are in a unique sense "church books" few will now deny. The church both provided the seedbed out of which they sprang and planted the seed. Individuals watered, fertilized, and pruned the growing plants, but not for personal advantage. The fruits were for all who belonged to the fellowship of believers and for any whom the Lord might call through

[3] *St. Mark* (7th ed.; London: Methuen & Co. Ltd., 1949), p. xviii.

his followers. The Gospels are practical, not "literary" works. They were used in the church's teaching, worship, missionary activities, discipline, and controversy with political and religious opponents.[4]

Estimates vary concerning the importance and effectiveness of each of the Gospels. J. A. Findlay has written, "It has long been my conviction that the 'Gospel according to Matthew' is the loveliest as well as the most important book in the world." [5] Morton Scott Enslin regards Mark as the "most important of our Christian records," as "the studied product of genius which, more effectively probably than we shall ever know, determined the pattern and character of early Christianity." [6] It is well known that Renan called the Gospel of Luke "the most beautiful book in the world." [7] William Temple, when he was Archbishop of York, expressed his preference for the Fourth Gospel in the words, "As long as I can remember I have had more love for St. John's Gospel than for any other book." [8] It belongs to the essential glory of the Gospels that each in its own way speaks movingly and intimately to the spirits of men.

Whatever may be the verdict of modern men concerning the relative value of the Gospels, it is evident that the Gospel of Matthew was the most read and valued in the early church. The careful research of Édouard Massaux on the influence of

[4] See Frederick C. Grant, *The Gospels: Their Origin and Their Growth* (New York: Harper & Brothers, 1957), pp. 11-38; Rudolf Bultmann, *Die Geschichte der synoptischen Tradition* (3. *Aufl.;* Göttingen, 1957); and Martin Dibelius, *From Tradition to Gospel* (New York: Charles Scribner's Sons, 1935).

[5] *Jesus in the First Gospel* (London: Hodder & Stoughton Ltd., 1925), p. 7.

[6] "The Artistry of Mark," *Journal of Biblical Literature,* LXVI (1947), 385, 392.

[7] *Op. cit.,* p. 283.

[8] *Readings in St. John's Gospel* (First and Second Series; London: Macmillan & Co. Ltd., 1945), p. vi.

this Gospel on Christian literature before Irenaeus (*ca.* A.D. 180) has shown clearly that it was the most often quoted and the most influential of all our New Testament writings in that period.[9] Early Christians turned to it again and again, particularly to the Sermon on the Mount, for guidance on the conduct of their lives and of the Christian community and for clarification of the relationship between the new law and the old. They were not so much interested in the deeds as in the words of Jesus. In these they found the norm for the Christian life. So influential was the Gospel of Matthew that Massaux can say that it "created the climate of ordinary Christianity" in this period.[10] Its position at the head of the New Testament canon probably reflects its dominance in early Christianity. At any rate, it is symbolical of it.

The Gospels in all probability have been studied more thoroughly than any other writings known to man, as a glance at Albert Schweitzer's *Von Reimarus zu Wrede* (1906) [11] and C. C. McCown's *The Search for the Real Jesus* (1940) will show. And still the work goes on. It will be the purpose of the remainder of this chapter to survey a few of the areas in the study of the Gospel of Matthew where scholars are now at work and to point out some of their interesting results. At least the questions they are asking about this Gospel will become apparent.

A Primary or a Secondary Gospel?

Augustine believed that Matthew was the earliest Gospel, that it was written in Hebrew and subsequently translated into Greek, and that Mark represents an abridgment of Matthew.[12]

[9] *Influence de l'Évangile de saint Matthieu sur la littérature chrétienne avant saint Irénée* (Louvain, 1950), pp. 647-55.

[10] *Ibid.*, p. 652.

[11] *The Quest of the Historical Jesus* (3rd Eng. ed.; London: A. & C. Black, 1954).

[12] *The Harmony of the Gospels* I.2.3-4.

In the second century Papias had written, "Matthew composed the Logia in the Hebrew language, and every one interpreted (translated?) them as he was able." [13] Whether Papias was referring to our canonical Gospel of Matthew or to one of its sources has been much debated.[14] But it is clear from these comments, the widespread use of Matthew in the early church, and the position it occupies in the order of the Gospels in the New Testament, that the early church regarded it as not only the first of the Gospels to be written but as the primary authority for information concerning Jesus. Mark was generally ignored during this period.[15]

Challenge to the ancient belief in the priority of Matthew resulted from careful investigation of the literary relations among the first three Gospels in the nineteenth century and the first quarter of the twentieth. Many scholars became convinced that Augustine and the early church were wrong—that Mark was written first and that Matthew is in some way dependent on Mark. In 1911 James Moffatt averred as a firm conclusion of New Testament research that "the priority of Mark to Matthew and Luke no longer requires to be proved." [16] The priority of Mark is widely affirmed in our time as the one fully established result of synoptic criticism.[17]

[13] Eusebius, *The Ecclesiastical History* III.39.16.

[14] See Benjamin Wisner Bacon, *Studies in Matthew* (New York: Henry Holt & Co., 1930), pp. 443-51. For a sketch of the relation of the Papias statement to attempted solutions of the synoptic problem see L. Vaganay, *Le problème synoptique* (Tournai, Belgium: Desclée, 1954), pp. 1-32, 51-4.

[15] Burnett Hillman Streeter, *The Four Gospels* (London: Macmillan & Co. Ltd., 1924), p. 10, comments thus: "It [Mark] is the Gospel least valued, least quoted, and most rarely commented on by the Fathers."

[16] *An Introduction to the Literature of the New Testament* (New York: Charles Scribner's Sons, 1911), p. 180.

[17] Sherman E. Johnson writes in *The Interpreter's Bible,* VII (Nashville: Abingdon Press, 1951), 235: "It may be considered settled, with as great certainty as one can ever achieve in literary criticism, that Mark is the principle source used by Matthew and Luke."

But the verdict was never quite unanimous. Two learned German Protestants of conservative bent, Theodor Zahn and Adolf Schlatter, long contended vigorously for the originality of Matthew and Roman Catholic scholars were held to the traditional position by the decisions of the Biblical Commission of June 19, 1911, and June 26, 1912.[18] Two important reinvestigations of the synoptic problem by Roman Catholics have appeared recently, both arguing for Matthean priority: B. C. Butler, *The Originality of St. Matthew* (1951) and L. Vaganay, *Le problème synoptique* (1954). An Episcopalian scholar, Pierson Parker, in a book entitled *The Gospel Before Mark* (1953), arrives at a position close to that of Augustine and the official Catholic view.

Since the investigation of the synoptic problem had slowed almost to a standstill following the appearance of B. H. Streeter's *magnum opus, The Four Gospels* (1924) and the shifting of interest, as a result of the work of the Form Historians, to the oral period lying behind the first written documents, the new flurry of interest in the synoptic problem is noteworthy. The confident assumption that the synoptic problem had been solved, at least in main outlines, is now being challenged vigorously. We are being aroused, as H. G. Wood has reminded us, from what John Stuart Mill has called "the deep slumber of a decided opinion." [19]

How vigorous the challenge is readily appears when one samples the temper of Butler's book. In attacking the dominant belief in the priority of Mark and the reasons lying behind it, Butler uses such terms as "vicious inference," and "school-

[18] For the text see John Chapman, *The Four Gospels* (New York: Sheed & Ward, 1944), pp. 75-83. For the effect of the decisions on Roman Catholic advocates of the priority of Mark see Francis J. McCool, S. J., "Revival of Synoptic Source-Criticism," *Theological Studies,* XVII (1956), 475 ff.

[19] "The Priority of Mark," *The Expository Times,* LXV (1953/54), 17.

boyish error of elementary reasoning." [20] He accuses his opposition of failure to keep an open mind. In short, he has introduced about as much heat as light into his discussion, an element unappreciated by such Protestant scholars as Allen P. Wikgren, of the University of Chicago, who decries his "startling invective." [21] Vaganay and Parker are considerably more modest, the former calling his results simply "a working hypothesis."

Some Protestants have praised Butler, notably Austin Farrer of Oxford, who has characterized Butler's book as "the most important discussion in English of the essentials of the two-document hypothesis since Streeter's *Four Gospels.*" [22] Vaganay's work has evoked a flood of articles and controversy, particularly within the Roman Church.[23] It is evident that ghosts long thought laid to rest are rising up to haunt us again.

What are the advocates of Matthean priority saying today about the origin of the Gospel of Matthew and about the synoptic problem as a whole? We can suggest their position only in general outline.

Basic is the contention that behind Matthew, Mark, and Luke lies a primitive Aramaic document, written by a Jewish Christian of Palestine (probably Matthew the apostle) well before the dispersal of the Jerusalem church and the destruction of Jerusalem. Butler is of the opinion that this Jewish-Christian document was used by the first apostles and missionaries as an aid to memory in their preaching and evangelization. Parker holds that its author insisted, after the

[20] *Op. cit.,* p. 63.

[21] In a review in *The Journal of Religion,* XXXII (1952), 219.

[22] In a review in *The Journal of Theological Studies,* New Series, III (1952), 102. Farrer is chiefly impressed by Butler's attack on Q. He does not agree with him on the originality of Matthew.

[23] Surveyed in detail in the article by McCool mentioned in note 18.

manner of the Jerusalem church, on strict obedience to the law, that he was opposed to the Gentile mission and hostile to the work of Paul and the somewhat liberal attitudes of Peter. He dates its writing to about A.D. 55, after the height of the Judaizing controversy. Vaganay thinks that Matthew simply wrote down the Jerusalem catechesis of Peter.

All agree that this primitive Palestinian document (we may call it "Proto-Matthew") was soon translated into Greek, which translation became the basic source of our Synoptic Gospels. Mark abridged it sharply, omitting its Judaistic sections and expanding certain parts of it by means of data received from the preaching of Peter. Butler goes so far as to suggest that it was really Peter who edited (orally) this Jerusalem source "to make it more palatable to his Gentile audience"[24] and that Mark simply recorded Peter's version of it.

There is difference of opinion whether Luke used the Greek "Proto-Matthew." Parker believes that he knew only the Marcan abridgment. Vaganay regards Mark as Luke's primary source, though he thinks Luke had the Greek "Proto-Matthew" as a secondary source.

The source of the triple tradition in the Synoptic Gospels is thus held by these scholars to be "Proto-Matthew" in Greek translation. But what about the double tradition, the passages usually designated as deriving from Q?

Here there is little exact agreement. Butler avers that "Q is a myth . . . an unnecessary and vicious hypothesis."[25] Luke simply copied from Matthew. In this Butler wins the resounding approval of Austin Farrer, who himself has attempted to overthrow the Q hypothesis (by force of words if not by arguments).[26] Vaganay holds that the so-called Q materials derive

[24] *Op. cit.*, p. 169.

[25] Pp. 118, 170.

[26] In the review cited in note 22 Farrer says flatly, "He [Butler] demolishes the Q hypothesis." For Farrer's attack on Q see "On Dispensing

from a Greek translation of an Aramaic sayings-collection, whose author is unknown but who may have been the apostle Matthew. From the first it was intended as a supplement on the sayings side for the Aramaic "Proto-Matthew." Parker accepts the Q hypothesis much as customarily formulated. He attempts to show that Q materials were added to the original Jewish-Christian Gospel by the compiler of our Gospel of Matthew. Luke also used this independent sayings source.

Butler regards our canonical Matthew, then, as a Greek translation of an Aramaic Matthew. It was abridged by Mark and copied in part by Luke. Vaganay and Parker see no such simple solution to the synoptic problem.

Vaganay regards our Greek Matthew as ultimately derived from the apostle Matthew's Aramaic Gospel but supplemented with sayings material and even influenced in places by Mark, a Roman version of the Greek translation of the primitive Aramaic Gospel. In addition to these sources the final author introduced material from sources available only to him, now appearing in the genealogy, the birth and infancy stories, the *testimonia,* additions to the passion and resurrection stories, and the like. Vaganay grapples more seriously with the complex data wrapped up in the synoptic problem than does Butler.

Parker joins arms with Butler and Vaganay in the main contention: that a primitive Aramaic Gospel, probably by the apostle Matthew, in Greek translation is the basic source of the Synoptics, and that Mark has abridged this. He departs from them in regarding Q as an independent sayings source used by Matthew and Luke, though Vaganay's "supplementary" sayings-source is not markedly different. Parker be-

with Q," in D. E. Nineham (ed.), *Studies in the Gospels* (Oxford: Basil Blackwell, 1955), pp. 55-86, which drew the comment from J. Jeremias, *temperamentvoll* and *nicht durchschlagend* (*New Testament Studies,* II [1955/56], 290). Vincent Taylor has recently reaffirmed his belief in Q in "The Original Order of Q," A. J. B. Higgins (ed.), *New Testament Essays* (Manchester Univ., 1959), pp. 246-69.

lieves that Matthew's peculiar materials, apart from some editorial revisions, come from "Proto-Matthew." This view anchors the virgin birth story and many of Matthew's unique additions to the passion and resurrection narratives in primitive Palestinian Christianity. In Parker's view the redactor of our present Gospel joined "Proto-Matthew" and Q together late in the tenth decade of the first century.

Now what have been the reactions to these attempts to establish the originality of Matthew in the face of the long dominant belief in the priority of Mark? Most Roman Catholic discussion has centered in the views of Vaganay. The controversy in the Roman Church has been admirably summarized and evaluated by Francis J. McCool, S. J.[27] McCool says that some scholars (e.g., L. Cerfaux of Louvain) agree in the main with Vaganay. Others (J. Levie, J. Schmid, A. Wikenhauser) have strongly opposed his views as a step backward, rather than forward, in synoptic criticism. He points out that from about 1890 until the decisions of the Biblical Commission in 1911 and 1912 many Catholic scholars were swinging toward the view that Mark and Q were the two basic sources of the Synoptic Gospels. Their researches were interrupted by a decision which compelled adherence to belief in the priority of the Gospel of Matthew, affirmed its original language as the native dialect of Palestine, fixed its author as the apostle Matthew, dated its composition before the destruction of Jerusalem, rejected the possibility that the apostle Matthew was the author only of one of its sources and that the present book was put together by a redactor, and asserted the substantial identity of the Greek translation and the Semitic original. Such a decision produced consternation in some scholarly circles in the Roman Church. However, there was no alternative but to adjust to it in so far as possible.[28]

[27] See note 18.

[28] This is admitted with amazing candor by Father McCool.

It is clear that some Catholic scholars are convinced that the only adequate answer to the synoptic problem lies in the direction of the two-source view: that the triple tradition rests on Mark and the double tradition on a Greek document other than Mark. They have adjusted to the decision of the Biblical Commission by attaching the name of Matthew to this second source, which they regard as a Gospel, not simply a collection of sayings.

How close this view is to the two-source position condemned in the decision of the Biblical Commission may be seen by comparing it with the views of B. W. Bacon in his *Studies in Matthew* (1930). In addition to Mark, as a basic source Bacon postulated a source S, consisting of the passages ordinarily assigned to Q and much other similar material with approximate, but not identical, parallels in Matthew and Luke. Bacon believed that S was a Gospel, with a Passion story, like the other Gospels. The only difference here is that Bacon did not attach the name of the apostle Matthew to this Gospel. Many of Bacon's critical views would, of course, be unacceptable to these Catholic scholars, such as his emphasis on the sweeping editorial freedom exercised by the redactor of our canonical Gospel. But in main outline the source theories are the same.

The extent of the revolt by liberal-minded Catholic scholars is evidenced in the support Father McCool finds from the researches of contemporary Protestant scholars: Vincent Taylor, C. H. Dodd, W. L. Knox, and N. A. Dahl. In an exciting way he finds common ground between Catholic and Protestant scholars, promise perhaps of better understanding and co-operation in the future. Belief in the priority of Mark and in the general outlines of the two-source theory is very much alive in some Roman Catholic circles.

Recent Protestant research has tended to confirm the priority of Mark. Krister Stendahl's study of the quotations from the Old Testament in the Gospel of Matthew has led him to conclude that the author of Matthew took quotations from Mark. He finds the hypothesis of an original Aramaic Matthew unacceptable.[29] N. A. Dahl, in a highly competent examination of Matthew's Passion narrative,[30] concludes that Matthew has reworked Mark's Passion story, adding to it materials derived from oral tradition and touching up the whole stylistically. He believes that the evidence indicates that the Gospel of Mark was known to the first readers of the Gospel of Matthew and that some of the alterations of Mark may have taken place in the community to which the author of Matthew belonged ahead of the compilation of his Gospel. He further affirms that the Gospels of Matthew and Luke were written independently. When they agree against Mark, it is likely that they both knew an oral tradition which had arisen around Mark. Dahl's chief contribution lies in his emphasis on the interplay between literary and oral traditions in the formation of the Gospel of Matthew. He declares himself against the views of the advocates of Matthean priority.

These observations may suffice to show that the citadel of Marcan priority, though heavily attacked in our time, has by no means capitulated. Even a respected group of Roman Catholic scholars is restive under the dictum affirming Matthean priority (and certain contemporary reaffirmations of it). That Mark is primary and Matthew secondary seems established.

A Jewish-Christian or a Gentile-Christian Gospel?

An inevitable corollary of the tradition recorded by Papias that Matthew wrote in the Hebrew language was the belief that his Gospel was written for Jewish Christians in Palestine.

[29] *The School of St. Matthew* (Uppsala, 1954), p. 155.

[30] "Die Passionsgeschichte bei Matthäus," *New Testament Studies,* II (1955/56), 17-32.

Irenaeus in the late second century declared that "Matthew among the Hebrews issued a Writing of the gospel in their own tongue." [31] Origen in the third century recorded the tradition that the Gospel of Matthew was "published . . . for those who from Judaism came to believe, composed as it was in the Hebrew language." [32] This view has persisted through the centuries and has advocates today, both Catholic and Protestant.

Two problems are involved. Was the author a Jewish or a Gentile Christian? And what can be said about the identity of the first readers?

The dominant view today is that both writer and readers were Jewish Christians. The general grounds for this judgment are said to be such data as: the presence in the book of a genealogy tracing Jesus' descent from Abraham, the strong interest in the fulfillment of Old Testament prophecy, the appearance of Semitic words and idioms, the lack of explanation of elements of Jewish piety (gift at the altar, Sabbath observance, almsgiving, fasting, prayer), the limitation of the mission of Jesus to Israel, the apocalyptic eschatology, the Jewish avoidance of the divine name in the phrase "the kingdom of heaven," and the high regard for the law and its scribal interpretation.

Some thirty years ago Ernst von Dobschütz [33] argued strongly that the author was a converted rabbi, who carried his intellectual and spiritual gifts into the service of the gospel. Von Dobschütz pointed to the love of stereotyping and formalizing in the Gospel (the repetition of words and phrases, the doublets, the schematic number arrangements), the presence

[31] *Against Heresies,* III, 1 (E. R. Hardy's translation).

[32] Eusebius, *The Ecclesiastical History* VI.25.4 (Lawlor's and Oulton's translation).

[33] "Matthäus als Rabbi und Katechet," *Zeitschrift für die neutestamentliche Wissenschaft,* XXVII (1928), 338-48.

of favorite rabbinic expressions and constructions, and the attitude toward the law and scribal interpretation. He remarked that specialists in rabbinic literature like best of all to work on the Gospel of Matthew. He even hazarded the suggestion that the author may have been a pupil of the famous rabbi Johanan ben Zakkai.

B. W. Bacon roundly seconded von Dobschütz's conclusions in his *Studies in Matthew* and carried the argument farther.[34] Bacon found Matthew's self-portrait in 13:52: a "scribe who has been trained for the kingdom of heaven." He believed that Matthew was not only a collector and schematic arranger of his sources but an author who rewrote his material freely, injecting into his narrative his peculiar "rabbinic" point of view. Bacon saw Matthew as deliberately patterning his Gospel after the five books of Moses and representing Jesus as a second Moses, the giver of a new and higher law as a fulfillment of the old law. The Christianity of Matthew was a new legalism, said Bacon, based on the words of Jesus rather than Moses; obedience to Jesus' teaching was held necessary for entrance to the kingdom of heaven.

Most interpreters since von Dobschütz and Bacon have been convinced that the author was a Jewish Christian, although not all have been sure that he was a converted rabbi.[35] G. D. Kilpatrick, in an important book entitled *The Origins of the Gospel According to St. Matthew* (1946), proceeds along many of the lines laid down by Bacon, including the assumed Jewish-Christian point of view of the author and readers. Günther Bornkamm contends strongly for the Jewish-Christian character of this Gospel.[36] His careful analysis of the theology of Matthew leads to the conclusion that Matthew and the church

[34] See especially Chapter X: "Traits of the Redactor."

[35] *E.g.,* Paul Feine and Johannes Behm, *Einleitung in das Neue Testament* (9. *Aufl.;* Heidelberg, 1950), p. 52.

[36] "Enderwartung und Kirche im Matthäusevangelium," in W. D.

for which he wrote had not yet left Judaism but were in process of separating because of the bitter attacks directed against them by the leaders of the synagogue. Official Judaism was anxious to suppress heretical sects, among which were the Christians. Bornkamm remarks that "the Messiahship of Jesus and the validity of his teaching are represented and defended throughout in the framework of Judaism. . . . The struggle against Israel is still a struggle *intra muros.*" [37] N. A. Dahl [38] holds that the breach between church and synagogue is somewhat farther along than the stage suggested by Bornkamm, that in fact the separation of the followers of Jesus from the Jews is complete. He agrees that the author and many members of his church were of Jewish origin, but affirms that they were not particularistic in their outlook. They had come to believe in the church universal. Dahl thus pictures the author and many of his readers as liberalized Jewish Christians who now saw that "the people of God of the new Covenant is the church from all nations." [39]

A minority opinion concerning the basic outlook and orientation of the Gospel of Matthew has been expressed by K. W. Clark [40] and Poul Nepper-Christensen.[41] The former points out

---

Davies and David Daube (eds.), *The Background of the New Testament and Its Eschatology* (Cambridge: University Press, 1956), pp. 222-60. This essay has been reprinted (with some changes) in Günther Bornkamm, Gerhard Barth, and Hans Joachim Held, *Überlieferung und Auslegung im Matthäusevangelium* (Neukirchen Kreis Moers, 1960).

[37] *Ibid.*, p. 36.

[38] *Op. cit.*, p. 28.

[39] *Ibid.* W. L. Knox (*The Sources of the Synoptic Gospels* [Cambridge: The University Press, 1953-7], II, 7) holds, however, that Matthew believed that the "many . . . from the East and the West" (Matt. 8:11) would enter the kingdom as proselytes, for "the Jewish law holds good for the new kingdom."

[40] "The Gentile Bias in Matthew," *Journal of Biblical Literature*, LXVI (1947), 165-72.

[41] *Das Matthäusevangelium—ein judenchristliches Evangelium?* (Aarhus, 1958).

that there is a Gentile, as well as a Jewish, bias in the Gospel of Matthew to be seen in: the denunciation of Pharisees and Sadducees (Ch. 23; 16:6); the emphasis on the definite and final rejection of Israel by God (8:12; 21:43); the Great Commission (28:19, 20); the general heightening of the miraculous in the Gospel; the story of the Virgin Birth; and various minor touches and emphases. He argues that Luke, a Gentile, also uses a genealogy and that Gentile Christians were accustomed to the use of scriptural proof-texts and prophecies and to Jewish eschatology. The Jewish particularism is due to the fact that the gospel material came out of Judaism and does not therefore reflect the attitude of the author of the Gospel. The Old Testament quotations are from the Septuagint, not the Hebrew text. But the author's Gentile bias is to be seen most of all in his oft emphasized assertion that God has finally rejected the Jews and accepted believing Gentiles as his people. No Jewish Christian would take this position. Paul, a convert from Judaism, clung to the hope that God would yet save the Jews (Rom. 9-11). The position taken in the Gospel of Matthew is more natural for a Gentile Christian than for a converted Jew.

Nepper-Christensen makes no attempt to establish the identity of the author. He is concerned with the question of the first readers, whether the early Christian tradition that the book was written in Hebrew for Jews or Jewish Christians can be sustained. He answers in the negative. In his judgment there are no clear marks that our present Gospel is a translation of a Semitic original and no evidence exists that early Christian Fathers (Papias, Irenaeus, Origen, Eusebius, Jerome) had ever seen the alleged Hebrew text. Furthermore, the characteristics of this Gospel do not suggest Jewish or Jewish-Christian readers. There is the same kind of interest in the fulfillment of prophecy in the Gospel of John, even to the use of "formula" introductions to quotations of the Old Testament

(John 13:18; 17:12; 19:24, 36). Gentile Christians, as well as Jewish ones, would find the concept of fulfillment meaningful. Typological interpretation of the Old Testament in the Gospel of Matthew does not differ significantly in kind and amount from that in the other Gospels. The so-called particularistic note (the limitation of the apostles to Jewish territory and the like) testifies to the historical facts of the first mission, not to the point of view of the original readers. The inclusive note at various points in the Gospel (8:11; 21:43; 24:14; 28:18-20) indicates the true outlook of the writer and readers. The fact that the Gospel of Matthew so soon became the most popular of the Gospels in the Gentile church argues against an original Jewish or Jewish-Christian destination.

The central argument against Jewish-Christian authorship advanced by Clark, namely, that no Jewish Christian would believe that God had finally rejected the Jews and accepted in their place the Gentiles, is treated at length by S. G. F. Brandon.[42] This writer emphasizes the profound effect of the fall of Jerusalem and the destruction of the Jewish nation on the thinking of both Jews and Christians. Questions of theodicy were inevitably thrust to the fore by this tragic event. The author of the Gospel of Matthew met the challenge of A.D. 70 with "a veritable philosophy of history." [43] The cause of the downfall of the Jews was their refusal to recognize Jesus for what he really was and to accept him. The Jews, who were rightfully the "sons of the kingdom" (Matt. 8:12), had been cast out and the Gentiles were taking their place. This was a fact, and Matthew simply came to terms with it when he thought deeply on the sovereign purpose of God in the light of an accomplished event.

[42] *The Fall of Jerusalem and the Christian Church* (London: SPCK, 1951), Ch. XII.
[43] *Ibid.*, p. 227.

Brandon believes that Matthew was not particularly happy about the Gentiles who were inundating the church, but he was reconciled to them. He wanted them to be robed with the "wedding garment," i.e., to live in the church on the right basis —respect for and observance of the law as interpreted by Jesus. He wished to counteract the antinomian influence of Paul. By exalting Peter as the head of the church and the keeper of the keys of the kingdom (16:17-19) he intended to exalt Peter's anti-Pauline view of the law. According to Brandon, there is no pro-Gentile bias in the Gospel of Matthew. Even the Great Commission charges the disciples to teach the Gentiles "to observe all that I have commanded you" (28:20), and this includes obedience to the "least commandments" of the law (5:19) and the decisions of the scribes and Pharisees (23:2, 3). For Brandon the Gospel of Matthew is Judaistic to the core; it represents Jerusalem Christianity as transplanted to Alexandria.

Nepper-Christensen's views have not yet been evaluated fully by scholars.[44] But a few comments may be ventured here. He is undoubtedly right in questioning the early church's tradition concerning the language (Hebrew) in which the Gospel of Matthew was believed written. No convincing case can be made for our Greek text as a translation of a Semitic original. The attempt of Butler, Vaganay, and Parker to establish the existence of an Aramaic "Proto-Matthew" is generally regarded to have failed, as we noted above. The Gospel of Matthew was probably originally written and read in Greek.

Nepper-Christensen seems to have underestimated the Jewish characteristics of the book. His coverage of the relevant data is limited, as he recognizes. By sampling here and there among the data, the impact of the "Jewish" characteristics (lit-

[44] See, however, W. D. Davies' review in the *Journal of Biblical Literature,* LXXIX (1960), 88-91, and Günther Bornkamm's remarks in *Überlieferung und Auslegung im Matthäusevangelium,* p. 47, note 2.

erary and theological) is considerably minimized. Furthermore, he does not see the data in the perspective of Jewish usage as he ought. His failure to grasp the full significance of the typological use of the second Moses ideology in Matthew is a case in point.[45] He seems to be right in viewing the particularistic elements of the Gospel as an inheritance from primitive tradition, not as evidence concerning the point of view of the readers. And his contention that the popularity of Matthew in the Gentile churches argues against an original Jewish-Christian destination seems cogent. As will be seen in Chapter V of this book, the present writer regards the author as a "Hellenist" of the same stamp as Stephen (Acts 6-7), thus as a Jewish Christian, who was writing in Greek for a mixed Gentile-Christian and Jewish-Christian community. He was not legalistic in his understanding of Christianity.

H. J. Schoeps, in his detailed study of Jewish Christianity,[46] while recognizing the Jewish-Christian marks in the Gospel of Matthew, yet affirms that it "represents emerging Catholicity and has as a whole no Judaizing tendency."[47] Its author, though a Jewish Christian, belongs in spirit and outlook to the "great Church." Near Schoeps stands N. A. Dahl, who, as we have said, stresses the universal outlook of the author. Of the same opinion is J. Jeremias, who writes: "Of the three synoptists Matthew evinces the strongest inclination to ascribe to Jesus a missionary activity among the Gentiles."[48]

Many scholars have contended that the readers of the Gospel of Matthew lived in Palestine.[49] Streeter argued for Antioch in Syria. Bacon thought the evidence pointed toward a Greek-

[45] See below, p. 124 ff.

[46] *Theologie und Geschichte des Judenchristentums* (Tübingen, 1949).

[47] *Ibid.*, p. 64.

[48] *Jesus' Promise to the Nations* (Naperville, Ill.: Alec R. Allenson, Inc., 1958), p. 34.

[49] E.g., Theodor Zahn, Julius Schniewind, and some Roman Catholic scholars.

speaking community of northern or northeastern Syria, the back country of Antioch, where large centers of Jewish population are known to have existed. Here where Greek was the standard tongue Aramaic persisted strongly in use and along with it Jewish-Christian traditions, which were used by the author of the Gospel of Matthew in supplementing and reworking the Greek Gospel of Mark. Bacon's views on the place of writing have been reiterated by J. Spencer Kennard.[50] A large and prosperous city of Phoenicia, perhaps Tyre or Sidon, is favored by Kilpatrick. Alexandria is proposed by Brandon. The only agreement that has been reached is that the Gospel came from some territory beyond or near the eastern end of the Mediterranean.

By way of summary, we may say that the weight of scholarship favors the view that the author was a Jew by birth and training, who had carried into the service of the church many features of his Jewish heritage. A growing number of recent scholars is impressed by his catholicity of outlook. He is the advocate of no narrow, particularistic Jewish Christianity but belongs in spirit to the "great church." The point of view of the first readers is not so clear. Discussion is going forward on their racial background and theological outlook. Some regard them as Jewish Christians who still bear a tenuous relationship to the synagogue; others as a mixed group, both Jewish and Gentile in origin, no longer connected, even nominally, with Judaism; and still others largely, if not entirely, Gentile Christians. There is no agreement concerning where they lived, other than that it was somewhere at or near the eastern end of the Mediterranean.

An Individual and/or a Community Product?

It was stated earlier in this chapter that a major emphasis

[50] "The Place of Origin of Matthew's Gospel," *Anglican Theological Review*, XXXI (1949), 243-46.

in New Testament scholarship of recent times concerns the role played by the Christian community in the creation of our Gospels.[51] The Gospels are "church books." The church perpetuated the memory of Jesus. It used his teachings in instructing converts concerning the meaning and demands of their new faith, in controversy with opponents, and in internal discipline. It recounted Jesus' deeds of mercy and act of redemption in its worship services and its evangelistic preaching. Through use the traditional material came to bear the stamp of the church's theology and total life.[52] The Gospels therefore tell us much about the church out of which they came, as well as about Jesus.

Until the rise of critical study of the Gospels it was assumed that in the Gospels of Matthew and John the personal recollections of apostles are recorded and that in the other two we are only one step removed from the apostolic circle. Stress was laid on the identity of the writers as a guarantee of the accuracy of their records. The new perspective has tended to thrust the writers into the background. Indeed, many scholars confess themselves unsure of the identity of a single one of the four Evangelists! And they are not particularly concerned about their lack of certainty, for they see that behind the four Gospels lies the witness not of four men but of the whole early church. That the Gospels are in a real sense social products, and there-

[51] P. 16 ff.

[52] The actual degree of creativity of the early church in the formation of the tradition concerning Jesus has been hotly debated. Opinion ranges from the somewhat radical views of Rudolf Bultmann (*op. cit.*), who assumes that the church is responsible for a considerable amount of the content of the Gospels, to the conservative estimate of H. Riesenfeld in *The Gospel Tradition and its Beginnings—A Study in the Limits of "Formgeschichte"* (London: A. R. Mowbray & Co., Ltd., 1957). The latter holds that the tradition from the first was "holy" and was passed along by accredited persons without the sort of reworking and expansion alleged by the Form Historians.

fore of even more value as sources of historical information, is widely accepted today.

This point of view must not be overdone, however. There are evidences of self-conscious literary activity, as, for example, in the Gospel of Luke.[53] And behind each of the Gospels must lie the mind of someone who gave to the traditional materials their present form.

The amount of freedom exercised by the writer of the Gospel of Matthew has been much discussed. Von Dobschütz and Bacon were inclined to stress it to a maximal point. The latter regarded Matthew as in every sense an "author," who rearranged and rewrote with complete freedom. The views of Sherman E. Johnson,[54] Frederick C. Grant,[55] and Günther Bornkamm[56] tend to stress the individual aspect of the work lying behind the Gospel.

On the other hand are those who point out that the peculiar features of this Gospel are due not so much to the work and idiosyncrasies of one man but to trends and emphases in the church to which he belonged. These scholars have attempted to discover the Gospel's *Sitz im Leben,* the precise elements in the church's life which have left their mark on the book.

G. D. Kilpatrick[57] and Philip Carrington[58] have advanced the thesis that the Gospel of Matthew exhibits characteristics of the church's liturgical life. The former points to the Jewish practice of reading the law and the prophets in the services of

[53] Streeter calls Luke "a consummate literary artist" (*op. cit.,* p. 548). Krister Stendahl writes: "Luke alone of the evangelists sets out to write literature and to maintain Hellenistic standards and the ideals of LXX Greek" (*op. cit.,* p. 32).

[54] In *The Interpreter's Bible,* VII (1951), 231-44.

[55] *Op. cit.,* Ch. XI.

[56] In *Überlieferung und Auslegung im Matthäusevangelium,* p. 47, note 2.

[57] *Op. cit.,* particularly Chapters IV and V.

[58] *The Primitive Christian Calendar* (Cambridge: The University Press, 1952), I.

worship, followed by a translation or paraphrase in the vernacular (Targum) and a homiletical exposition of the Scripture. He notes the tendency of expositions of Scripture in the synagogue to become Scripture themselves (as in Baruch and the Epistle of Jeremy). Likewise, Christians of the second century read from the Old Testament and various other edifying books (such as I Clement, the Shepherd of Hermas, the letters of Ignatius). In Kilpatrick's opinion the Gospel of Mark and the sources Q and M were read repeatedly (for more than twenty years) in the church to which Matthew belonged, and around these documents grew up a fixed element of exposition along the lines of Jewish *Haggadah* and *Halakah*. Somewhere between A.D. 90-100 the Gospel of Matthew appeared as "a kind of revised gospel book, conveniently incorporating into one volume the three documents Mark, Q, and M." [59] Kilpatrick thinks it "natural that, in a revised gospel book produced for the worship of the Church, the needs and convenience of liturgical practice should be consulted." [60] He thus finds three factors in the composition of the Gospel of Matthew: the sources, liturgical usage, and editorial activity.

As evidence that the Gospel of Matthew was written to be read aloud in church, Kilpatrick points first to the writer's abbreviation and simplification of Mark's narratives. These alterations he regards as made in the interest of better auditory understanding. Matthew's explanatory additions, the carefully balanced and rounded phrasing, the repetition of formulas and sayings (doublets), and the removal of crudities of Mark's style he sees as evidence of liturgical purpose. Certain portions of the Gospel seem to him once to have comprised homiletical materials; they now occupy places alongside sections they were originally designed to interpret. And he thinks that the orderly arrangement of materials implies that the writer wished to

[59] *Op. cit.*, p. 70.
[60] *Ibid.*

make his book useful for exposition. It is obvious that this explanation of the origin of the Gospel of Matthew spreads considerably the responsibility for the unique features of the book.

Carrington's views run along the same general lines as Kilpatrick's. However, he attempts more precision in the liturgical analysis of the Gospel material. Carrington's primary interest is in the Gospel of Mark, which he thinks was written as a lectionary. Its sections are believed by him to have been designed for reading in the church in successive seasons of the Christian year. These sections he attempts to identify. He regards the Gospel of Matthew as an enlarged lectionary, following in its main divisions the pattern in Mark.

Carrington's and Kilpatrick's researches have been subjected to searching analysis by W. D. Davies [61] and Krister Stendahl [62] respectively. Many of Davies' criticisms of Carrington are applicable also to Kilpatrick. Davies warns against inferring that the lectionary practice of the synagogue was simply taken over by the church. He argues for a much more fluid concept and practice of worship in the primitive church and contends that the New Testament as a whole does not support the view that the early church followed a liturgical calendar as closely as this hypothesis suggests. And that Mark and Matthew were put together expressly so that they could be read in units appropriate to the seasons of the Christian (and Jewish) year seems to him an hypothesis imposed on the documents. He is willing to grant that the liturgical practices of the church influenced the transmission of the Gospel tradition, but not in such mechanical ways as Carrington, at least, assumes.

[61] "Reflections on Archbishop Carrington's *The Primitive Christian Calendar*" in W. D. Davies and David Daube (eds.), *The Background of the New Testament and Its Eschatology* (Cambridge: The University Press, 1956), pp. 124-52.

[62] *Op. cit.*, pp. 20-23.

In short, it appears that the church's use of the Gospel tradition in worship has affected the form in which this tradition appears in our Gospels, but precisely how has not yet become clear.

A different *Sitz im Leben* for the Gospel of Matthew is pointed out by Krister Stendahl and Gottfried Schille.[63] Both see Christianity, from its beginning in Jesus, as a "school," in which the gospel was learned. Jesus was a teacher and his disciples learners. The early "ministers of the word" (Luke 1:2), to which group Mark belonged (Acts 13:5),[64] were teachers who passed on to others the mysteries of the kingdom of heaven as imparted by Jesus, the basic content of the church's memory of Jesus, and the meaning of Jesus' words and deeds for the life of men. Schille believes that these teachers attempted to think through and deepen the church's basic faith, to relate it to the Old Testament and the purposes of God in history.

Stendahl finds a close connection between the study and instructional emphasis in primitive Christianity and in the Qumran community. He attempts to establish a basic similarity between the type of Old Testament interpretation in vogue at Qumran (as seen especially in the Habakkuk Commentary) and the use of the Old Testament in the formula quotations[65] of the Gospel of Matthew. He argues that this Gospel's major features reflect scholarly interest and activity in the early church of a kind like that in the "school" at Qumran.

[63] Stendahl, *op. cit.;* Gottfried Schille, "Bemerkungen zur Formgeschichte des Evangeliums. Rahmen und Aufbau des Markus-Evangeliums," and "Das Evangelium des Matthäus als Katechismus," *New Testament Studies,* IV (1957/58), 1-24 and 101-14.

[64] On the meaning of ὑπηρέτης see B. T. Holmes, "Luke's Description of John Mark," *Journal of Biblical Literature* LIV (1935), 63-72, and Stendahl, *op. cit.,* pp. 32-33.

[65] Matt. 1:23; 2:6, 15, 18, 23; 4:15-16; 8:17; 12:18-21; 13:35; 21:5; 27:9-10. Each possesses an introductory formula and all are without synoptic parallels.

Stendahl's "School of St. Matthew" is a school for teachers and church leaders, not for catechumens. Schille, on the other hand, believes that parts of the Gospel of Matthew (such as the Sermon on the Mount) consist of pre-baptismal catechetical material and that the whole Gospel bears the stamp of the church's catechetical tradition. Stendahl settles on a school for teachers and church leaders, rather than for catechumens, because of the interest in the Gospel of Matthew in disciplinary procedures (especially in 18:10-35), which information, he thinks, would be superfluous for catechumens. Comparison with the Didache and the Manual of Discipline of the Qumran community leads him to the conclusion that our Gospel is a manual or a handbook for teachers and church leaders. A major interest of this school was to understand how the prophecies of the Old Testament were fulfilled in Jesus and the church. In this understanding principles of interpretation like those in use in the "school" at Qumran were employed.

A thorough evaluation of Stendahl's attempt to establish the *Sitz im Leben* as a "school" has been made by Bertil Gärtner.[66] Gärtner maintains that the similarities between the use of the Old Testament at Qumran and in the Gospel of Matthew have been overstressed by Stendahl, that in fact the differences actually overshadow the similarities. Matthew was seeking to show how the prophecies were fulfilled in a historical personage, Jesus, while the Qumran community was interested in the signs of the times, how world periods were running their course and the age of fulfillment dawning. The Teacher of Righteousness is given no such central place in prophetic fulfillment as is Jesus. Gärtner holds that the attempt in the Gospel of Matthew to prove that Jesus fulfills the messianic prophecies of the Old Testament reflects more nearly the

[66] "The Habakkuk Commentary (DSH) and the Gospel of Matthew," *Studia Theologica,* VIII (1954), 1-24.

church's missionary preaching in Jewish synagogues than a "school" *Sitz im Leben*. He is willing to grant that in this Gospel the intellectual or "school" emphasis is represented. The teachers of the Christian community must have possessed a tradition of messianic passages "as a sort of 'memory-tradition,' "[67] but the use of these passages arose originally in missionary preaching. The upshot of Gärtner's criticism is that Stendahl has not proved from the formula quotations and the supposed parallel to the Qumran type of interpretation that the background of this Gospel is a "school," though this may be held possible on other grounds.

Worship, teaching, and preaching have thus been suggested as the *Sitz im Leben* for the Gospel of Matthew. But is it not possible that all have played their part in the creation of the Gospel? Can it be doubted that the material of this Gospel would lend itself to use in worship, teaching (including pre- and post-baptismal instruction, if both existed in the primitive church,[68] and counsels for church leaders and administrators), and missionary preaching? Would not this material serve to build up the life of the church within, help the church to defend itself against attacks from without, and advance its claims concerning Jesus to those beyond its fellowship? Is the Gospel of Matthew "a kind of omnibus volume,"[69] a potpourri of elements from many sides of the church's life and meant to nourish these many sides? If this Gospel became *the* Gospel in that area of the church in which it appeared,[70] was its manysidedness

[67] *Ibid.*, p. 23.

[68] Schille (*op. cit.*, p. 102 f.) argues that both existed at the beginning but that the post-baptismal *catechesis* soon dropped out. Stendahl thinks the question undecided. See his citation of the relevant literature (*op. cit.*, p. 22, note 5).

[69] W. D. Davies' characterization of Carrington's conception of this Gospel as a combination of liturgical sources (*op. cit.*, p. 126).

[70] Streeter, *op. cit.*, pp. 9 ff.

part of the explanation for its success? Such questions have yet to be answered definitively.

Some problems in the field of Matthean studies and some tentative answers have now been reviewed. Let us recapitulate briefly and draw out a few implications.

As of the present, it appears that the long accepted conclusion concerning the priority of Mark will stand the attacks of the advocates of Matthean priority. If the Gospel of Matthew rests firmly on the Gospel of Mark, it is hardly possible to argue that its author (or compiler) was the apostle Matthew. Mark was not an apostle. Would an eyewitness like Matthew depend so largely for his material on an "outsider" like Mark? And are the kinds of alterations made in Mark's material (to be pointed out in part in the chapters to follow in this book) understandable on the hypothesis that the author of the Gospel of Matthew was an apostle? It appears not. But the apostle Matthew conceivably may be responsible for some source (possibly Q) used by a later compiler or for some traditions (probably oral) included in the Gospel. The church obviously believed that his witness to Christ somehow lay behind this writing.

That the Gospel was written by a Jewish Christian seems established. On the grounds of style and theology one might argue that the author was a converted rabbi, though this position falls considerably short of certainty. Whether the first readers were Jewish Christians, Gentile Christians, or both has not been settled. They seem not to have been narrow legalists of an exclusive spirit. It would appear that their separation from the synagogue was complete. The church believed that God's wrath had fallen on the synagogue and the Jewish nation in the catastrophe of A.D. 70, because of the Jews' rejection of Jesus. The future of the church lay in the Gentile world. Its role now was to baptize Gentiles in the name of the Father,

Son, and Holy Spirit and to teach them to observe all that Jesus had commanded (Matt. 28:20).

Where the Matthean church was located and exactly when the book was written are obscure. Perhaps the strongest case has been made for Syria or Phoenicia. The variety of locations suggested, however, shows how inconclusive the data are. The use of Mark (written probably between A.D. 65-70) and the quite obvious allusion to the fall of Jerusalem in A.D. 70 [71] place the time of writing somewhat after that date but probably before the end of the first century.[72]

It is clear that this Gospel is a "church book." It grew in part out of the life of the church and was meant to minister to its needs. The author has taken traditional materials, as they had been used and interpreted in his and other communities, and arranged and edited them in line with his own outlook and interests. These probably varied only little from the characteristics that marked his community as a whole.

Exactly what needs in the life of the church the book was meant to serve will become apparent in the chapters to follow.

[71] Matt. 22:7, where the burning of the city (not mentioned in Luke's version of the parable) seems a direct allusion to this event. See Brandon, *op. cit.*, p. 227.

[72] Streeter dates the Gospel to c. A.D. 85. He points out that some fifteen passages in the letters of Ignatius (c. A.D. 115) look like reminiscences of the Gospel of Matthew. Bacon and Kilpatrick find the period A.D. 90-100 as most satisfactory for the time of the writing of the Gospel.

[2]

The Basis of Jesus' Authority

In a recent book Vincent Taylor remarks, "Jesus will always remain a challenge to be met rather than a problem to be solved." [1] By this he means that we can never hope to snare Jesus in the net of our minds. Jesus is about as unencompassable as the Milky Way. But we keep weaving larger nets in the hope that we can ensnare one star at least.

The writers of the New Testament were aware of their inability to comprehend the mystery of Jesus' person. The author of Ephesians wrote about "the love of Christ which surpasses knowledge" (3:19), and expressed the hope that both he and his readers, under the ministrations of Spirit-endowed men, would "attain to the unity of the faith and of the knowledge of the Son of God" (4:13). They knew that they saw "in a mirror dimly" (I Cor. 13:12) and they longed for the day when they would "see him as he is" (I John 3:2). They too kept making larger nets.

The great variety of New Testament titles applied to Jesus testifies to the inadequacy of any one way of representing him. To use another figure, the old wine skins (such as Rabbi, Prophet, Messiah, Son of David, Son of Man, Lamb of God,

[1] *The Person of Christ in New Testament Teaching* (London: Macmillan & Co. Ltd., 1958), p. 166.

High Priest, Savior, Servant, Lord, Word) simply cannot hold the new wine. He bursts them all and leaves the wine merchant in frantic search of better containers. Jesus will always remain a pursuit rather than a possession.

The widely divergent ways of characterizing Jesus in the New Testament have some common roots. One of them is suggested by the word "authority" (ἐξουσία). Though Paul and the author of the Gospel of Matthew differ in many respects theologically, the former would agree with the latter, and indeed with all other New Testament writers, in the Christological affirmation contained in Jesus' post-resurrection words as recorded in Matt. 28:18: "All authority in heaven and on earth has been given to me." [2] E. G. Selwyn has shown recently how basic to the whole New Testament the emphasis on the authority of Jesus is, as evidenced, for example, by the importance attached to Jesus' sayings in the primitive church and the prevalence of the title "Lord" as applied to him.[3]

Matthew in particular is interested in setting forth Jesus' authority for the church of his day. Several scholars rightly have pointed to Matt. 28:18-20 as the key passage of this Gospel.[4] Here many of the emphases of the book are caught up: (1) the absoluteness and all-embracing character of Jesus' authority ("all authority in heaven and on earth"); (2) its derivative character ("has been given to me"); (3) the command to evangelize all nations ("make disciples of all nations");

[2] *Cf.* Phil. 2:9-11; I Cor. 15:24-28.

[3] "The Authority of Christ in the New Testament," *New Testament Studies,* III (1956/57), 83-92.

[4] Oscar Cullmann, *Königsherrschaft Christi und Kirche im Neuen Testament* (Zürich, 1950), p. 10; Otto Michel, "Der Abschluss des Matthäusevangeliums," *Evangelische Theologie,* X (1950/51), 21; E. Lohmeyer, "Mir ist gegeben alle Gewalt," in Werner Schmauch (ed.), *In Memoriam Ernst Lohmeyer* (Stuttgart, 1951), pp. 22-49; Gottfried Schille, "Bemerkungen zur Formgeschichte des Evangeliums. II. Das Evangelium des Matthäus als Katechismus," *New Testament Studies,* IV (1957/58), 113.

(4) the definition of the nature of discipleship (baptism in the name of the Father, Son, and Holy Spirit and the observance of all that Jesus has commanded); (5) the assurance of Jesus' presence until the close of the age ("I am with you always, to the close of the age").[5]

Matthew's portrait of Jesus centers in his representation of Jesus' authority. Mark before him was interested in the same theme. Matthew reproduces Mark's passages in which Jesus' authority is emphasized;[6] adds the narrative concerning the authority of the Capernaum centurion, which indirectly highlights Jesus' authority (8:5-13); comments independently that Jesus "cast out the spirits with a word" (8:16); introduces a whole series of "But I say to you" sayings, whose effect is to dramatize Jesus' authority (5:21-48); represents Jesus as a second Moses, who gives his new Torah from a mountain;[7] repeatedly affirms that Jesus is the Messiah and Son of God, to whom the Father has delivered all things, especially a unique revelation of himself (11:25-27); and holds up Jesus as the coming Son of Man whose verdict will admit or exclude from the kingdom of heaven (25:31-46). The statement on Jesus' lips at the very end of the Gospel—"All authority in heaven and on earth has been given to me"—simply catches up the thrust of the entire story.

The term "authority" (*ἐξουσία*) has a long history and a varied usage in classical and Hellenistic Greek. It is derived from a word meaning "it is allowed," "it is possible" (*ἔξεστιν*) and has as its primary meaning "power of choice," "liberty of

[5] Points 1-4 are treated in the materials to follow in this book. Point 5 may be buttressed by referring to Matt. 18:20, a verse peculiar to this Gospel. *Cf.* 1:23.

[6] Mark 1:22—Matt. 7:29; Mark 2:10—Matt. 9:6; Mark 6:7—Matt. 10:1; Mark 11:28, 29, 33—Matt. 21:23, 24, 27. Matthew does not have Mark 1:27, for he omits Mark 1:23-8 (or perhaps telescopes it with the story of the Gadarene demoniac—Streeter, *op. cit.*, p. 170).

[7] See pp. 124 ff.

action." In contracts, wills, and other legal documents of the New Testament period it denotes the "claim," or "right," or "control" one has over anything. It comes to mean also "ability to do something, capability, might, power" and is thus descriptive of the power exercised by rulers and officials of various sorts.[8]

In the Septuagint of Dan. 4:17 God ("the Lord of Heaven") is said to have authority (ἐξουσία) over all things in heaven and on earth and to do whatever he wills with them. The meaning of the term with respect to Jesus is well suggested in Selwyn's paraphrase of Mark 1:22: "He taught them like a sovereign and not as the Rabbis." [9] The authority of Jesus as set forth in the Gospel of Matthew is clearly *sovereign* authority: "All things have been delivered to me by my Father"; "All authority in heaven and on earth has been given to me." This latter passage directly reflects Dan. 7:14 in the Septuagint where it is said of the one like a son of man: "And authority (ἐξουσία) was given to him; and all the nations of the earth in every race and every dignitary serve him. And his authority is an eternal authority."

"Authority" as both inherent right and manifest capability usually is associated with particular identity: one has it because of what or who he is or what he is made to be by another. Such authority is a concomitant of status. What is Jesus' status, as Matthew sees it?

Jesus as the Messiah

We have noted already that Matthew represents Jesus' authority as derived from God, his Father. Here he is at one

[8] James H. Moulton and George Milligan, *The Vocabulary of the Greek Testament* (London: Hodder and Stoughton Ltd., 1952), p. 225, and Walter Bauer (trans. William F. Arndt and F. Wilbur Gingrich), *A Greek-English Lexicon of the New Testament and Other Early Christian Literature* (Chicago: University of Chicago Press, 1957), p. 277.

[9] *Op. cit.*, p. 86.

with New Testament Christology as a whole. Even in the Fourth Gospel, where Jesus' deity is so strongly stressed, it is insisted that Jesus' authority comes from the Father. The Father has sent him. He speaks the words of God and does God's works. He lives in complete obedience to the will of God, in a relation of absolute dependence. The Father has delegated to him, as the Son, divine powers and prerogatives.[10]

The Messiah of Jewish hope was always pictured as God's representative, empowered by God and acting in his behalf. This figure has been much studied of late.[11]

Mowinckel concludes that the conception of the Messiah in Judaism has its roots in the old royal ideology of Israel, which represents a modification under the influence of Yahwism of Canaanite and Babylonian king-concepts. In the Israelite ideal the king as Yahweh's adopted Son was regarded as both human and divine. Through anointing and Spirit-empowerment he had been elevated above his fellows as the representative of God to the people and of the people to God. As God's chosen and appointed instrument he was to be completely subordinate to Yahweh and he was to become the channel of God's covenant blessings to Israel. He was to reign in righteousness (i.e., in accordance with God's standards of justice), to deliver Israel from her enemies, to maintain peace and prosperity in the land. As the official leader in the national cultus he was to intercede and sacrifice for the people and become the channel through which God's blessings were mediated to them.[12]

[10] C. H. Dodd, *The Interpretation of the Fourth Gospel* (Cambridge: University Press, 1953), pp. 254 ff.

[11] Sigmund Mowinckel (tr. George W. Anderson), *He That Cometh* (Nashville: Abingdon Press, 1956); Aage Bentzen, *King and Messiah* (London: Lutterworth Press, 1955); Helmer Ringgren, *The Messiah in the Old Testament* (London: SCM Press, 1956); Aubrey R. Johnson, *Sacred Kingship in Ancient Israel* (Cardiff: University of Wales, 1955); Joseph Klausner (tr. W. F. Stinespring), *The Messianic Idea in Israel* (New York: Macmillan & Co., 1955).

[12] Whether Israel, like Egypt and Mesopotamia, ascribed divinity to

Israel's ideal of kingship was of course never realized historically. The hope that an ideal king would come must have been accentuated by the death of every faithless monarch and the anointing of each successor. The hoped-for ideal king, so far as we can see from the Old Testament, was not called "the Messiah." This is a technical term that arose in the intertestamental period for an eschatological figure (or figures) whose role was to put into effect God's final purposes for mankind.[13]

When Israel fell before the Assyrians and the Babylonians and national life came to an end, the conditions were at hand for the rise of the messianic hope. Israel's kingly ideal was now projected into the future. In the intertestamental period and subsequently the hope for a coming deliverer took many forms.

In the dominant popular form the Messiah was thought of as a human being from the line of David, divinely appointed and endowed but nonetheless human. He is pictured clearly in the Psalms of Solomon, a Pharisaic work of about 45 B.C. Here God is besought to raise up for Israel "their king, the son of David," who will "shatter unrighteous rulers" and "purge

its kings has been much debated. Engnell, Mowinckel, and Bentzen see some participation by Israel in the sacral king ideology of the ancient East. The view that the concept of charismatic leadership distinguished Israel from her neighbors (and that the king therefore was not regarded as divine) has been supported by Albrecht Alt, "Das Königtum in den Reichen Israel und Juda," *Vetus Testamentum,* I (1951), 2 ff., and Martin Noth, "Gott, König, Volk im Alten Testament," *Zeitschrift für Theologie und Kirche,* XLVII (1950), 157 ff. Henri Frankfort, *Kingship and the Gods* (Chicago: University of Chicago Press, 1948), pp. 337-44, thinks Israel regarded the king as simply a glorified chieftain without any particular sanctity.

[13] It appears in the Qumran texts, The Damascus Document, the Psalms of Solomon, I Enoch, and other intertestamental books. On the two-Messiah concept see Karl Georg Kuhn, "The Two Messiahs of Aaron and Israel," in Krister Stendahl (ed.), *The Scrolls and the New Testament* (New York: Harper & Brothers, 1957), pp. 54-64.

Jerusalem from nations that trample (her) down to destruction," who will himself be "pure from sin" and "gather together a holy people, whom he shall lead in righteousness." The nations will come from the ends of the earth "to see his glory." "He will smite the earth with the word of his mouth for ever." In his great, God-given wisdom "he will bless the people of the Lord with wisdom and gladness," "shepherding the flock of the Lord faithfully and righteously." His authority, power, wisdom, and righteousness are said to derive from God. He is called "the anointed of the Lord." [14] The role of the Messiah portrayed in these Psalms is both political and religious.

The Qumran community by the Dead Sea hoped for two Messiahs, one from Aaron (priestly) and the other from Israel (political).[15] The leading role was to be played by the priestly Messiah. Neither appears to have been thought of as in any sense divine. The subordination of the political to the priestly Messiah seems to indicate that these sectarians thought of Israel's future more in religious than in political terms.

A third form is to be seen in the Son of Man expectation, known to us from the apocalypse called I Enoch. Here the future deliverer is a supernatural figure hidden away with God in heaven. He will come to judge the world, open the kingdom to the righteous, and destroy the wicked.[16]

In some quarters of Judaism in New Testament times the Messiah clearly was thought of as a second Moses. The first great deliverer from bondage and the giver of the law had

[14] Psalms 17 and 18; R. H. Charles' translation (*The Apocrypha and Pseudepigrapha of the Old Testament,* II, Oxford, 1913). Mowinckel regards this conception of the Messiah as the view of the masses, although to some extent also of the upper classes.

[15] See the article by Kuhn mentioned in note 13 and Millar Burrows, *More Light on the Dead Sea Scrolls* (New York: The Viking Press, 1958), Ch. XXVI.

[16] See below, pp. 70 ff.

been glorified extravagantly. Philo of Alexandria viewed Moses as king, lawgiver, high priest, and prophet and virtually deified him. It was believed that, like Elijah and Enoch, he had been taken up into heaven and that he would return at the beginning of the messianic era as eschatological prophet or possibly as the Messiah. Some thought the Messiah would be the prophet like Moses mentioned in Deut. 18:15, 18. It was believed that events of the Mosaic period would be re-enacted in messianic times.[17]

Yet another form appears in the Messiah ben Joseph (or Ephraim) expected by Jews of the second century. He was thought of as a warrior Messiah, who would precede the appearance of the more religious or spiritual Messiah ben David.[18]

Joseph Klausner points out that the messianic concept throughout its history had a dual character: on the one hand, it stressed "politico-national salvation"; and, on the other, "religio-spiritual redemption." "These two elements walked arm in arm. The Messiah must be both *king* and *redeemer* . . . he is the great political and spiritual hero at one and the same time." [19] Klausner declares that no *Jewish* Messiah, for all his spirituality, could be imagined as saying what Jesus is reported to have said, "My kingdom is not of this world" (John 18:36). It is evident from these comments that the Messiah as a heavenly king and judge, as portrayed in I Enoch, is quite exceptional and even unJewish.[20]

The Gospels make it clear that Jesus had little sympathy with the politico-national aspects of the messianic role. In the wilderness he rejected the suggestion of Satan that he fulfill such expectations. When he was acclaimed as "Messiah," he

[17] See below, pp. 124 ff.
[18] Joseph Klausner, *op. cit.*, pp. 483-501.
[19] *Ibid.*, p. 392.
[20] See below, p. 71.

sought to counter the ascription, apparently because of its political connotations, and to stop its spread among the people.[21] It is possible that as many as four or five of the Twelve had formerly belonged to the Zealot movement and were eager to have Jesus assume leadership in the cause of rebellion against Rome.[22] When the multitude wanted to force him into the kingship, he withdrew to the hills to thwart their purpose and possibly to pray for divine guidance and strength (John 6:15). Though he rode into Jerusalem in apparent fulfillment of a messianic prophecy, he seems to have wanted to say thereby that he came as a king of peace, not of war. Even if Mark is correct in representing him as admitting his messiahship to the high priest,[23] he quickly redefined his role as that of the Son of Man, a title for which he had a distinct preference. It is ironical that he should have been crucified as a Zealot by the Romans.[24]

That Jesus saw himself as fulfilling a high role in the purpose of God seems quite beyond dispute. He believed that he was the coming one (Matt. 11:2-6), that in him God's final purposes for Israel and the nations were being carried out. Since he was conscious that he was God's eschatological deliverer, he could neither wholly deny that he was the Messiah so long expected, nor could he accept the role without serious qualification or reinterpretation. He preferred other and better characterizations of his mission—those which were wholly or practically devoid of politico-economic connotations. He could accept half

[21] Mark 1:25, 34; 3:12; 8:29 ff.; Luke 4:41. See George Duncan, *Jesus, Son of Man* (New York: The Macmillan Co., 1949), Ch. X.

[22] Oscar Cullmann, *The State in the New Testament* (New York: Charles Scribner's Sons, 1956), pp. 14 ff.

[23] For the opposite view see Oscar Cullmann, *Die Christologie des Neuen Testaments* (Tübingen, 1957), pp. 118 ff.

[24] Oscar Cullmann, *The State in the New Testament,* Ch. II.

of the dual role involved in the messianic idea, as defined by Klausner, but not the other part.[25]

In spite of Jesus' reservations about the term and the role it suggested, soon after his death the word Messiah became firmly attached to his name. According to the book of Acts (2:36) Peter on the day of Pentecost affirmed that God had made Jesus "both Lord and Christ." "Christ" is simply the Greek equivalent for the Hebrew "Messiah." Paul refers many times in his letters to "Jesus Christ" and sometimes to "Christ Jesus." It is evident that in early Christian vocabulary the title was on the way to becoming a proper name, although its basic meaning seems not to have been quite forgotten.[26] The term has outstripped all others in the history of the church as a designation for Jesus.

It was acceptable to the first Christians, of course, only because its meaning had been reinterpreted by them. Jesus ap-

[25] The precise content of Jesus' self-consciousness has been much debated. Rudolf Bultmann (*Theology of the New Testament,* I [New York: Charles Scribner's Sons, 1951], 26-32) holds that Jesus regarded himself not as Messiah ("eschatological ruler") or Son of Man ("the heavenly judge and salvation-bringer") but as a prophet, rabbi, and exorcist, whose task was to proclaim the near advent of the kingdom of God and urge men to prepare to enter it. Frederick C. Grant (*The Gospel of the Kingdom* [New York: The Macmillan Co., 1940], pp. 126-127) asserts that Jesus made no high claims for himself but simply pointed to the God of power, love, and mercy who would soon bring in his kingdom. Leroy Waterman (*The Historical Jesus* [New York: Exposition Press, 1955], Ch. X) sees Jesus as consciously reviving the religion of the prophets and deliberately avoiding messianic and apocalyptic titles and roles. Against these relatively "low" estimates of Jesus' self-consciousness stand the majority of recent and contemporary scholars (e.g., William Manson, T. W. Manson, Martin Dibelius, Millar Burrows, Sigmund Mowinckel, Rudolph Otto, Oscar Cullmann, Joachim Jeremias, C. H. Dodd, Vincent Taylor, Werner G. Kümmel, Reginald H. Fuller). These scholars hold that Jesus saw himself as in some sense the inaugurator and ruler of the kingdom of God, that he was conscious of the final arrival of the eschatological salvation in his person and work.

[26] Cullmann, *Die Christologie des Neuen Testaments,* p. 112.

parently had laid the basis for such reinterpretation. He had tried to teach the Twelve that the Son of Man would suffer and pour out his life for "many." [27] So far as we are aware, he was the first in Judaism to define the Messiah's work in terms of the suffering Servant concept of Isaiah 53.[28] It appears that the disciples before the resurrection were unable to grasp his radically new teaching. But in the light of the Easter event and the consequent certainty of his exaltation to the right hand of the Father as reigning Lord, they saw clearly that it was "necessary that the Christ should suffer . . . and enter into his glory" (Luke 24:26).

Paul gloried in his preaching of a crucified Messiah, even though he knew full well that it was offensive to Jews and Gentiles alike (I Cor. 1:23, 24). In his suffering and death the Messiah, God's Son, had identified himself with sinful, dying humanity and in his glorious resurrection God had broken the hold of the powers of evil over his Son and those whom he had come to save. "When he ascended on high he led a host of captives" (Eph. 4:8). He was Messiah not in spite of his ignominious death but precisely because of it. His sovereignty was seen by the church not as parochial but ecumenical, his kingdom not the land of Israel but the whole universe (Phil. 2:9-11; Matt. 28:18; Rev. 5:13).

The term "Christ" appears in the Gospel of Matthew sixteen or seventeen times,[29] under three forms: Jesus Christ, the

[27] Mark 8:31 ff.; 10:45. The authenticity of the latter saying has been heavily attacked. Vincent Taylor (*The Gospel According to St. Mark* [London: Macmillan & Co., 1952], pp. 445-46) reviews the evidence and adjudges it favorable to authenticity.

[28] But see W. H. Brownlee's views in "Messianic Motifs of Qumran and the New Testament," *New Testament Studies,* III (1956/57), 12-30, 195-210, and the reaction of Millar Burrows (*The Dead Sea Scrolls* [New York: The Viking Press, 1955], p. 267, and *More Light on the Dead Sea Scrolls* [New York: The Viking Press, 1958], pp. 66, 316 ff.)

[29] In 16:21 some MSS have "Jesus Christ" and others "Jesus."

Christ, and Christ. The author's liking for this designation is evident from the fact that not more than five of his sixteen or seventeen instances are to be attributed to his sources Mark and Q.[30] Four or five seem to have been inserted into the narrative by him.[31] The rest lie in the material peculiar to his Gospel. It has long been recognized that this peculiar matter reflects the author's point of view.[32] Not only does he like the term but it obviously retains its basic meaning for him, since in only three places does it appear in the form "Jesus Christ," where it might be taken as a proper name.[33]

Matthew's attempts to prove that Jesus actually is the Messiah of the Jews are rather obvious to careful readers of the Gospel.

First, he makes it clear that Jesus was descended from David. Such descent was a requisite in the nationalistic form of the messianic hope. "Son of David" appears in the Psalms of Solomon (17:23) as a designation of the Messiah. In Mark 12:35 it is said that the scribes hold that the Messiah will be the son of David. In the second century and later "Son of David" occurs frequently not only as a descriptive title but as a personal name for the Messiah.[34]

That Jesus meets this basic requirement is shown in part by the genealogy which opens the Gospel of Matthew. The genealogy is artificially built up into three groups of fourteen

[30] 16:16; 22:42; 24:23; 26:63 from Mark and possibly 11:2 from Q.
[31] 16:20, (21?); 24:5; 27:17, 22.
[32] Sir John Hawkins, *Horae Synopticae* (Oxford: Clarendon Press, 1899), pp. 8-9; Benjamin Wisner Bacon, *Studies in Matthew,* pp. 120-42, 505-10.
[33] In 1:16; 27:17, 22 "Jesus who is called Christ" is paralleled in 4:18 and 10:2 by "Simon who is called Peter." Thus, in the former passages we are on the borderline between a title (an epithet) and a proper name.
[34] Joseph Klausner, *op. cit.,* p. 461; Hermann L. Strack and Paul Billerbeck, *Kommentar zum Neuen Testament aus Talmud und Midrash* (München, 1922-56), I, 525.

generations, the whole construction being perhaps a kind of numerical acrostic on the name "David." [35] The numerical value of the Hebrew letters in this name is fourteen. Thus the whole genealogy spells out thrice the name "David."

That Jesus is the Son of David is repeatedly asserted by those who in this Gospel address him: two blind men (9:27), a Canaanite woman (15:22), two blind men at Jericho (20:30, 31), the crowds (21:9), children (21:15). It is significant that in the first three of these instances Jesus is portrayed as responding to the belief in him represented by this form of salutation and as granting requests. Once (12:23) the crowd is made to query, "Can this be the Son of David?" In a later chapter[36] it will be shown that the multitudes are represented predominately in this Gospel as not fully understanding who Jesus is. However, such recognition as they do give adds to the effectiveness of the presentation of Jesus as the Son of David.

Secondly, the author stresses repeatedly that in Jesus the prophecies of the Old Testament find their fulfillment. His supernatural birth (1:22), incidents of his early life (2:5, 15, 17, 23), his ministry in Galilee (4:14), his work of healing (8:17), his desire to avoid publicity (12:17), the failure of his hearers to understand (13:14), his use of parables (13:35), his entry into Jerusalem (21:4), his betrayal (26:24), the desertion of his disciples (26:31), his arrest (26:54, 56), the use of the betrayal money (27:9)—all are said to have been predicted in the Old Testament. Whatever explanation one may give of Matthew's freedom in reproducing the text of the Old Testa-

[35] George H. Box, "The Gospel Narratives of the Nativity and the Alleged Influence of Heathen Ideas," *Zeitschrift für die neutestamentliche Wissenschaft,* VI (1905), 85.

[36] Pp. 101 ff.

ment,[37] it is clear what his central aim is: to prove that Jesus is the Messiah of Jewish expectation.

Thirdly, Jesus, the Messiah, is portrayed as fulfilling the role of the second Moses. This concept in the Gospel of Matthew will be treated in detail later,[38] but here it may be noted that in life experiences, teaching, and works the parallels between Jesus and Moses are drawn out in some detail. As babies both escaped death at the hands of wicked kings. Both came out of the land of Egypt. Both were tempted in the wilderness. Both fasted forty days and forty nights. Like Moses Jesus declared the will of God from a mountain. Like Moses he performed ten miracles. B. W. Bacon argued that the five great sections of teaching materials, with their narrative introductions, in the Gospel of Matthew are meant to suggest that Jesus, after the example of Moses, gave the new law in five books.[39] Whether this is true or not, the authority of Jesus in this Gospel is the authority of the one like Moses who is yet greater than Moses.

Matthew, in common with the other writers of the New Testament, is unabashed by the suffering and death of the Messiah. He sees these as the fulfillment of the will of God. Jesus' death is for "the forgiveness of sins" (26:28). His name is *Jesus,* "for he will save his people from their sins" (1:21). His death is necessary for the fulfillment of Scripture (26:54). The author pictures the Messiah as gladly accepting the way of suffering and inviting his disciples to take it too. The meekness and humility of the Messiah is a prominent feature of this Gospel.[40]

But death is not the end. Our author shows that God's

[37] See Krister Stendahl, *The School of St. Matthew, passim,* and the literature referred to there.

[38] Pp. 124 ff.

[39] See pp. 132-33.

[40] Gerhard Barth in Bornkamm, Barth, and Held, *op. cit.,* pp. 117 ff.

Messiah rose from the grave triumphant over death, the sealed tomb, and the guard of soldiers, and appeared in Galilee to his disciples as the heavenly Lord, invested by the Father with full messianic authority (Ch. 28). He is no longer king-designate; he is fully enthroned and awaiting only the end of the age for the establishing of his kingdom (28:18-20). His authority is universal.

Jesus as the Son of God

A second way of setting forth the basis of Jesus' authority in the Gospel of Matthew is to be seen in a group of phrases which portrays Jesus as the Son of God. Jesus is represented as speaking numerous times of "my Father" or "my Father in heaven" in a way that implies a unique relationship to God; and he is called "Son" or "Son of God" in a number of passages.

The term "Father" with reference to God occurs in Matthew some forty-five times. Seventeen of these appear as "my Father," often with the modifiers "heavenly" or "who is in heaven." Eighteen times "your Father" (often with the above modifiers) occurs. "Our Father" appears only once—in the Lord's Prayer. Found also are the vocative "Father" (two times), "the Father" (five times), "his Father" (once), and "their Father" (once). In Mark "Father" occurs only four times, and in Luke fifteen.

Two observations may be made. First, the term "Father" in some form appears in Matthew more than twice as often as in Mark and Luke together. Many of these usages apparently came from his special source. But that the author of this Gospel liked the term is evident. Mark 3:35 is changed from "whoever does the will of God" to "whoever does the will of my Father in heaven" (Matt. 12:50). In 20:23 Matthew adds to Mark's "for whom it has been prepared" (Mark 10:40) the phrase "by my Father." In Matt. 26:29, Mark 14:25 is changed from "in the kingdom of God" to "in my Father's kingdom." [41]

"Father" is also a favorite designation of God in the Fourth Gospel, where it occurs on the lips of Jesus some 107 times. Various scholars have shown that Jesus actually used the term sparingly, not profusely as the Gospels of Matthew and John represent.[42] But in the church the term before long became a metonym for God and as such worked its way profusely into the tradition of his sayings.[43] There can be no doubt that Jesus did speak of God as "Father," often meaning "my Father" in a special sense.[44] But it is evident that "Matthew and John . . . proclaim from the housetops what, in the more primitive documents, is whispered in the ear." [45]

Secondly, the frequent differentiation in the Gospel of Matthew between "my Father" and "your Father" and the single occurrence of "our Father" leads one to suspect that the author wished to emphasize Jesus' unique relation to God.

To the Jews of Matthew's time "my Father" was regarded as a phrase which only a particularly worthy person would take on his lips. The disciples of Rabbi Gamaliel II (*ca.* A.D. 90) in a time of distress at sea asked their master to pray for them. He did so, saying: "Our God, have mercy upon us!" Whereupon the disciples remarked that their master was worthy to unite

[41] T. W. Manson holds that the author of the Gospel of Matthew has six times introduced the term "Father" into Q sayings (*The Teaching of Jesus* [Cambridge: University Press, 1931], p. 100).

[42] T. W. Manson, *ibid.*, Chapter IV; Joachim Jeremias, "Abba," *Theologische Literaturzeitung*, LXXIX (1954), 214; Vincent Taylor, *The Person of Christ in New Testament Teaching*, pp. 174 ff.

[43] See the table of its usage in books of the New Testament other than the Gospels in Manson, *op. cit.*, p. 99.

[44] Jeremias has shown that *'abba* is a diminutive form of an Aramaic word which stems from the speech of little children, and that Jesus made bold to use this term of endearment in address to God. Jeremias thinks this usage unprecedented (see article referred to in note 42). *Cf.* G. Dalman, *The Words of Jesus* (Edinburgh, T. & T. Clark, 1902), p. 192.

[45] Manson, *op. cit.*, p. 100.

the name of God with himself. The Rabbi then prayed again and said, "*My* God, have mercy upon us." [46]

The author of the first Gospel obviously regarded God as the Father of Jesus in a sense in which he was not the Father of the disciples.

The unique relationship between Jesus and God is further highlighted in this Gospel by the use of the expressions "the Son" and "the Son of God." The author's liking for this way of relating Jesus to God is readily apparent. He introduces from Hosea a quotation by which Jesus is declared to be God's Son (Matt. 2:15). He represents God as publicly attesting Jesus' Sonship at the baptism ("*This* is my beloved Son"—3:17, whereas Mark has, "*Thou* art my beloved Son"—1:11). He introduces a passage from Q which stresses the unique relationship between Jesus and the Father ("no one knows the Son except the Father, and no one knows the Father except the Son"—11:27). In two parables the sonship of Jesus is stressed: the Wicked Husbandmen (21:33-43) and the Marriage Feast for the King's Son (22:1-14).

The latter parable varies markedly from its parallel in Luke 14:16-24. There the banquet is given by "a man," not by "a king" as "a marriage feast for his son." In Matthew the rejection of the invitation leads to the king's destruction of the city, a transparent allusion to the fall of Jerusalem in A.D. 70. This is obviously viewed as punishment for Israel's rejection of God's Son.

At the end of the Gospel the disciples are exhorted to "make disciples of all nations, baptizing them in the name of the Father and of the Son and of the Holy Spirit" (28:19). Here the Son has a place alongside the Father and the Holy Spirit in a kind of loosely conceived trinity.

"Son of God" is applied to Jesus in some form nine times in

[46] Strack-Billerbeck, *Kommentar zum Neuen Testament aus Talmud und Midrash* (München, 1922-56) I, 410.

the Gospel of Matthew. Four times the word "Son" has no article, while the word "God" does (4:3, 6; 8:29; 27:40); three times neither word has the article (14:33; 27:43, 54); and twice both words have the article (16:16; 26:63). Is there any difference of meaning among the three forms?

The problem comes into focus in such a passage as Matt. 27:54, where the Revised Standard Version has the centurion cry out, "Truly this was a son of God!"

E. C. Colwell, in a study of the use of the article in the Greek New Testament,[47] has gathered data which make it appear likely that in all the above phrases we should translate "the Son of God." His grammatical conclusion is in part that when predicate nouns without the article precede the verb such predicate nouns are nonetheless definite. "Son of God" (without the article) precedes the verb in Matt. 27:54; thus it should be translated, "Truly this man was the Son of God!" Precisely the same construction occurs in Matt. 14:33, where the Revised Standard Version translates rightly, "Truly you are the Son of God."

It will not do to remark, as Frederick C. Grant does,[48] that "a son of God" is the only plausible confession to come from the lips of a pagan. We have no right to assume, without question, that Matthew has preserved the *ipsissima verba* of this centurion and that we have only to ask what a Roman centurion likely would have meant by such a phrase. We have rather to ask concerning the rules of Greek grammar and what Matthew meant by it. On the latter point our clue is 14:33, where the disciples obviously are represented by Matthew as confessing Jesus as "the Son of God."

Assuming that the Gospel of Matthew wishes to say em-

[47] *Journal of Biblical Literature,* LII (1933), 12-21. Colwell is supported by C. F. D. Moule, *An Idiom Book of New Testament Greek* (Cambridge: The University Press, 1953), pp. 115-17.

[48] *The Gospel of Matthew* (New York: Harper & Bros., 1955), II, 57.

phatically that Jesus is "*the* son of God," what precisely does this mean?

The phrase "Son of God" had a long history and diversified usage in the world of our author's day.[49] In Judaism it was used as a characterization of Israel (Ex. 4:22; Hos. 11:1; Isa. 1:2; Jer. 3:22), of angels (Gen. 6:2; Job 1:6; 38:7), of the reigning king (II Sam. 7:14; Ps. 2:7; 89:27), of the righteous person (Sirach 4:10; Ps. Sol. 13:8; 17:30; 18:4), and possibly of the Messiah, though the evidence here is inconclusive. In the Gospels "Son of God" appears as a messianic term (Mark 14:61; Matt. 16:16; Luke 1:32), but material is lacking from Jewish sources to prove such usage in Judaism.[50]

In Semitic idiom "son of" expresses affinity or likeness. One calls to mind such phrases as: "a son of light," "a son of peace," "sons of thunder," "a son of Gehenna," "the son of perdition," "the sons of this age," "sons of the resurrection." "To share or express the quality of a thing was to be a 'son' of that thing." [51] Against this background a "son of God" would be one who is like God, who expresses in his life the character and being of God.

J. Bieneck has shown that the term in the Old Testament implies not the divine descent of the one (or ones) so designated but the peculiar call to service and obedience and the love of God for him (or them). To be a son and to serve are synonymous, says he.[52] Vincent Taylor, after a review of the

[49] See J. Bieneck, *Sohn Gottes als Christusbezeichnung der Synoptiker* (Zürich, 1951); G. P. Wetter, *Der Sohn Gottes* (Göttingen, 1916); Vincent Taylor, *The Names of Jesus* (New York: St. Martin's Press, 1953), pp. 52-65.

[50] See Taylor, *op. cit.*, pp. 53 ff.

[51] C. J. Wright in Major, Manson, and Wright, *The Mission and Message of Jesus* (New York: E. P. Dutton & Co., 1938), p. 681.

[52] For the reference see note 49. He does not deny absolutely the influence of the divine-king ideology of the ancient Near East on Israel's king concept, but he thinks it of considerably less importance than Engnell and his followers make it. He prefers to follow Baudissin's sug-

data, concludes: "The significance of the phrase in Jewish thought is reasonably clear: it does not describe a divine being, but characterizes groups or individuals who stand in a peculiarly close religious relationship with God." [53]

Quite a different connotation attends the usage of the phrase in the Hellenistic world. There kings long had been believed to be sons of the gods. Roman emperors frequently were thus hailed. Worship was in many places directed toward emperors, both dead and living. Roving prophets appeared in the syncretistic religions of the period and gave themselves out as sons of God or incarnations of God. Men with unusual powers of many sorts were acclaimed by the use of this term. Ernst Lohmeyer has summarized the situation in the Hellenistic world by saying that "son of God means to the Gentile every unusual human being from the philosopher to Caesar." [54] In that world the term meant divine descent, which descent was attested by unusual powers and capabilities.

If Jesus used the term as descriptive of his self-consciousness and sense of mission, as he seems occasionally to have done,[55]

---

gestion that the king in Israel was regarded as the "Spitze des Volkstums," the representative of the people (*op. cit.*, p. 54).

[53] *Op. cit.*, p. 54.

[54] *Das Evangelium des Markus* (Göttingen, 1937), p. 347.

[55] Rudolf Bultmann (*Theology of the New Testament* [New York: Charles Scribner's Sons, 1951-55], I, 28, 32) holds that Jesus did not think of himself as the "Son of God" but that this term was first applied to him after the resurrection by the earliest Jerusalem church. It arose as a result of a messianic interpretation of Ps. 2 and its application to Jesus. He holds further that nearly all of the passages in the Gospels where Jesus is named "Son of God" reflect the theology of the Hellenistic church and are of no value for understanding the mind of Jesus. Reginald H. Fuller (*The Mission and Achievement of Jesus* [Naperville, Ill.: Alec R. Allenson, Inc., 1954], pp. 80 ff.) argues that, while the evidence for Jesus' use of the term as a self-designation "is meager in the extreme," his use of "Father" in a unique way and the evidence provided by the stories of the baptism and temptation of Jesus (which surely rest on Jesus' own recollection shared with the disciples) make it reasonable to

there can be little doubt that his Jewish background largely shaped its content. It must have expressed his sense of peculiar closeness to God, of God-likeness, his complete acceptance of the divine will and eschatological service marked out for him, and his total response to God's love. As only (unique) [56] Son, he was to serve his Father in the fulfillment of the Father's redemptive purposes for the world.

That Jesus was confessed as "the Son of God" by the primitive Palestinian Christian community seems likely. However, supporting texts are few and of uncertain value. The term occurs only twice in Acts. Here the use is attributed to Paul only (9:20; 13:33) and in non-Palestinian settings. It is possible that in Rom. 1:3-4 Paul is quoting a traditional formulation concerning Jesus as God's Son.[57] Here it is said that he was "descended from David according to the flesh and designated Son of God in power according to the Spirit of holiness by his resurrection from the dead." If the passage goes back beyond Paul, it would seem to indicate that the primitive church believed that Jesus was the Son of God in weakness during the days of his flesh but that at the resurrection he became the Son of God "in power," that is, he became reigning Lord at that time, no longer subject to the limitations of the flesh. Oscar Cullmann thinks that one of the earliest Christian baptismal confessions was, "I believe that Jesus Christ is the Son of God." [58]

---

conclude that Jesus knew himself to be the Son of God in a unique sense. But he did not claim this status publicly: "Sonship means to Jesus not a dignity to be claimed, but a responsibility to be fulfilled" (p. 84).

[56] The Greek word (ἀγαπητός) translated in the RSV of Mark 1:11 by "beloved," really means "only," "sole." See Vincent Taylor, *The Gospel According to St. Mark,* p. 161.

[57] See Franz-J. Leenhardt, *L'épitre de saint Paul aux Romains* (Neuchatel, 1957), p. 22, and the literature there cited.

[58] *Baptism in the New Testament* (London: SCM Press, 1950), p. 71.

Apart from the Gospels the New Testament writings in which Jesus' Sonship is most stressed are the letters of Paul, the Fourth Gospel, I and II John, and the book of Hebrews. In view of the obviously large interest in the doctrine of Jesus' Sonship in the Hellenistic church, it is not strange that some scholars assume the doctrine arose and received its distinctive content there and was retrojected upon Jesus in the Gospels. But not all relevant passages can be charged to the early church. Mark 13:32, which admits a limitation in the Son's knowledge, surely was not created by the church, and many scholars are now willing to grant the essential authenticity of the saying in which Jesus as Son claims unique knowledge of the Father (Matt. 11:25 ff.—Luke 10:21 ff., a Q passage).[59]

We turn now to the content of the term in the Gospel of Matthew. Our best clues come from three passages: 14:33; 16:16 ff.; 28:18-20, with supplementary insight from the birth story.

In 14:33 Matthew presents quite a different picture from that given in the parallel passage of Mark (6:51-52). In Mark the disciples are portrayed as unresponsive to the great miracle of the walking on the water. They are unperceptive and hard of heart. In Matthew a wondering confession of faith appears: "Truly you are the Son of God." We have here Matthew's answer to the question propounded after the stilling of the tempest (8:27). The disciples there are made to query, "What sort of man is this, that even winds and sea obey him?" Mark and Luke have, "Who then is this . . . ?" Matthew is interested in explaining how it happens that Jesus can work miracles like these—"what sort of man" he is. He answers: he is "the Son of God"; and he says that the disciples worshiped him.[60]

[59] Reginald H. Fuller, *op. cit.*, pp. 89-95; Vincent Taylor, *The Names of Jesus*, pp. 60-64; J. Bieneck, *op. cit.*, pp. 75-87.

[60] The Greek word translated "worshiped" here (προσκυνέω) occurs thirteen times in Matthew but only twice in Mark and three times in

Plainly the meaning here is that Jesus was regarded by the disciples as a divine being. In this passage we come closer to the Hellenistic "Son of God" concept (a divine being who accredits himself as such by charismatic phenomena) than anywhere else in the Synoptic Gospels.

In 16:16 ff. Peter is made to declare Jesus not only the Christ (as in Mark and Luke) but also "the Son of the living God." That this is not simply a synonym for "the Christ" is evident from its meaning in 14:33. Peter's knowledge is then attributed to special revelation from the Father in heaven. Flesh and blood can never perceive who Jesus really is. Since Jesus belongs to the world of deity, only deity can know the truth about him. Here the point of view is close to Mark's, where only the demons know Jesus' true identity (Mark 1:24, 34; 3:11-12; 5:7).

The third significant passage (Matt. 28:18-20) calls to mind another, strikingly similar (Matt. 11:25 ff.). In fact, Matthew's post-resurrection logion may represent his comment on the Q passage recorded in 11:25 ff.

It would help our understanding of the mind of the author of the First Gospel if we could determine what, if any, changes he made in the Q passage when he incorporated it into his Gospel. Harnack thought these could be identified,[61] but scholars

---

Luke. A high degree of reverence is plainly indicated in the appearances of the word in Matthew. The wise men come to worship the babe (2:2, 11); Herod wants to worship him (2:8); those who come to Jesus in faith express their knowledge of his high status and are said to worship him (8:2; 15:25); and subsequent to the resurrection he is worshiped by the women at the tomb (28:9) and by the disciples (28:17). While the word is sometimes used of honor paid to a human being (*cf.* Matt. 18:26), it is most often used in Greek literature of worship of a supernatural or divine being.

[61] *The Sayings of Jesus* (New York: G. P. Putnam's Sons, 1908), pp. 272-310.

are no longer sure. The tendency now is to assume that Matthew's form represents substantially what stood in Q.[62]

That Matthew understood the implications of the Q saying appears from 16:16 ff. and 28:18-20. The Father's knowledge of the Son and his willingness to reveal this knowledge is stressed in both 11:25 ff. and 16:16 ff. The Father's delegation of authority to the Son is in view in both passages. In both, Father and Son are thrown together into the same absolute, unique relationship. The phrase "heaven and earth" of 11:25 is repeated or echoed in 28:18. The Son's yoke or commands are alluded to in both. B. W. Bacon believed that Matthew adapted 11:27 ff. to the form of a post-resurrection commission.[63] We cannot be sure that Matthew consciously adapted the Q saying, but we may say, at least, that 28:18-20 reflects the interpretation of the Q saying one would expect Matthew to make.

It appears from the passages we have considered that Matthew regarded Jesus as the Son of God during his earthly life. He believed that both Jesus and the disciples were aware of this. It had been revealed to the disciples by the Father. The unbelieving and untaught of God could not know who he really was.[64] During his earthly days he was Son of God incognito to those outside. After the resurrection and exaltation he was enthroned by the Father. Full authority as judge of all men and king over the created order had been given him. At the close of the age (28:20) this authority would be made known to all men (25:31 ff.). At the moment, as a result of his resur-

[62] See the works cited in note 59 and also J. Schniewind, *Das Evangelium nach Matthäus* (8. *Aufl.;* Göttingen; 1956), pp. 148-55. However, P. Winter ("Matthew XI 27 and Luke X 22 from the First to the Fifth Century," *Novum Testamentum,* I [1956], 112-48) supports Harnack's conclusion that "no one knows the Son except the Father" (Matt. 11:27) was not originally contained in Q.

[63] *Jesus, the Son of God* (New Haven: Yale University Press, 1911), p. 3.

[64] See below, pp. 99 ff.

rection and exaltation, he occupied a place alongside the Father and the Holy Spirit. When he appeared to the disciples on a mountain in Galilee, he was endowed with all the attributes of deity. Had not God so come on a mountain in times of old? Had he not come with his word of command to Israel? So God, the Son, comes to his disciples, the new Israel, with his authoritative word. And the disciples fall before him in worship (28:17). We can agree with Lohmeyer that the Christology here is as exalted as that reached in the Fourth Gospel.[65]

In the birth story Matthew attempts to explain how Jesus, the Son of God, came into being. He affirms that Mary conceived through the instrumentality of the Holy Spirit, and that the child was born in fulfillment of prophecy: "His name shall be called Emmanuel," "God with us" (1:23). The Jesus of Matthew is throughout "God with us."

Jesus as the Son of Man

A third term by which the basis of Jesus' authority in the Gospel of Matthew is indicated is "the Son of Man." This term occurs thirty-one times in this Gospel. Elsewhere in the Gospels, it almost always appears in sayings attributed to Jesus.[66] As we shall see, "the Son of Man" was a favorite designation of Jesus by the author of the First Gospel.

The question of the origin and meaning of "the Son of Man" has been much discussed.[67] On linguistic grounds it is now tolerably clear that the term *bar nasha* in Aramaic, the native

[65] "Mir ist gegeben alle Gewalt," in W. Schmauch (ed.), *In Memoriam Ernst Lohmeyer* (Stuttgart, 1951), p. 47.

[66] Only rarely in the New Testament is Jesus called "the Son of Man" by another—by the crowd in John 12:34 and by the dying Stephen in Acts 7:56. *Cf.* also Rev. 1:13; 14:14.

[67] E. Sjøberg, *Der Menschensohn im Aethiopischen Henochbuch* (Lund, 1946), pp. 40 ff.; John Wick Bowman, "The Background of the Term 'Son of Man,'" *Expository Times,* LIX (1947/48), 283-88; M. Black, "The 'Son of Man' in the Old Biblical Literature," and "The 'Son of Man' in the Teaching of Jesus," *Expository Times,* LX (1948/49), 11-15, 32-36; Sig-

language of Jesus, meant basically "the man," i.e., an individual of the species man. It is generally believed today that the term also could have borne the sense "the Man," in other words, that it may have carried a special emphasis.

In the Old Testament the corresponding Hebrew expression *ben adam* means "man" or "mankind," with special nuances here and there. In Ps. 8:4 "son of man" clearly means mankind in creaturely weakness and yet in nobility as the highest of God's creatures. In some ninety occurrences in Ezekiel the phrase carries the meaning mortal man or "mere mortal," whom God wills to lift up and strengthen with his Spirit. In an extremely important usage in Dan. 7:13 the Aramaic phrase "one like a son of man," characterizing the figure who comes with the clouds of heaven and appears before the Ancient of Days, means simply "a humanlike one."[68] Here the context (7:18, 27) shows conclusively that this humanlike figure, who as such stands in contrast to the beastly world powers around Israel, is a symbol for "the saints of the Most High," i.e., for the people of Israel. He is not the Messiah, an angel, one of the Amesha Spentas of Zoroastrian religion, or some other mythological figure.[69] In this passage God is represented as giving the kingdom (the sovereignty of the world) to humane Israel.

The Son of Man appears in subsequent Jewish literature (I Enoch,[70] IV Ezra, the Syriac Apocalypse of Baruch, and some of the Targums) in varying characterizations.

---

mund Mowinckel, *He That Cometh,* pp. 346 ff.; Oscar Cullmann, *Die Christologie des Neuen Testaments,* pp. 138 ff.; A. J. B. Higgins, "Son of Man—*Forschung* since 'The Teaching of Jesus,'" in A. J. B. Higgins (ed.), *New Testament Essays* (Manchester: University Press, 1959), pp. 119-35.

[68] James A. Montgomery, *A Critical and Exegetical Commentary on the Book of Daniel* (New York: Charles Scribner's Sons, 1927), pp. 317 ff.

[69] On the various identifications that have been made, see Montgomery, *ibid.*

[70] Critical controversy has long raged over I Enoch. Some have held

In the parables section of I Enoch (Chs. 37-71) a heavenly figure called "the Son of Man" (and frequently "this . . ." or "that Son of Man") is characterized at great length. He is pictured as a divine, pre-existent being, dwelling in heaven with the Lord of Spirits (46:1 ff.). His countenance is described as having "the appearance of a man," his face as being "full of graciousness, like one of the holy angels." It is said that righteousness dwells with him, that he reveals all the treasures of that which is hidden, that he has been chosen by the Lord of Spirits before the creation of the world, that he is to be a staff to the righteous, a light to the Gentiles, and the hope of those who are troubled of heart, that he will sit on God's throne and pour forth all the secrets of wisdom and counsel, that he will slay all sinners with the word of his mouth, and that unto him is committed all judgment. He will sit on the throne of his glory, destroy sinners from the face of the earth and bind and imprison them "in their assemblage-place of destruction," but he will be the savior and vindicator of the elect. Of these it is said, "And with that Son of Man shall they eat and lie down and rise up for ever and ever" (62:14). He is called also "His [God's] Anointed" (i.e., the Messiah—48:10; 52:4), "the

---

the whole book to be of Christian origin. Sjøberg, *op. cit.*, pp. 3 ff., has shown this to be quite impossible. More serious is the contention of J. T. Milik and others that the parables section (Chs. 37-71) may be the work of a Jewish-Christian writer. Possible evidence for this is the fact that no fragments of this section of the book were found at Qumran along with pieces from other parts of the work (J. T. Milik, *Ten Years of Discovery in the Wilderness of Judaea* [Naperville, Ill.: Alec R. Allenson, Inc., 1959], pp. 33 ff.). This, of course, is inconclusive, as fragments may yet turn up or the parables section may originally have comprised a separate (Jewish) book, possibly unknown or unrepresented at Qumran. The present writer, in view of the total lack of distinctive Christian emphases in the parables section, is inclined to follow Sjøberg in rejecting the hypothesis of a Christian origin. On the suggestion that the Son of Man passages are interpolations into the parables section (which is as a whole Jewish), see Sjøberg's refutation (pp. 11 ff.).

Righteous One" (38:2; 53:6), "the Elect One" (40:5; 45:3, 4; 49:2, 4, and others).

Rudolph Otto [71] affirms that this strange supernatural figure of the Son of Man—a functionary between God and the orders of angels and men, reserved in heaven until the day of judgment, when he will vindicate the righteous and destroy the wicked—certainly did not originate in Israel. In Daniel the "one like a son of man" represents the people of Israel. It has been thought by some that the Son of Man in I Enoch is likewise a symbol for the elect community. But this is clearly impossible.[72] We are dealing here with a supernatural savior, who, though he stands in intimate relationship with his people ("the elect") is nevertheless distinguished from them. He is appointed by God to be their deliverer and shepherd and the judge of their oppressors. In some respects he resembles the Messiah of Jewish politico-national expectation; but in others he is more like the saviors of Iranian or Indo-Iranian myths.[73]

It has become increasingly clear that the Son of Man concept, as set forth in I Enoch and other apocalyptic books,[74] roots not in Old Testament theology but rather in oriental-Hellenistic religio-philosophical speculations concerning a divine Primordial Man (*Urmensch* or god *Anthropos*). The cosmos was thought of as existing originally in human form. From this human form (Primordial Man) both the world and the souls of men emanated and to this form they will return at the last. Primordial Man is really a deity, the son of the supreme god, endued with divine glory. He is thought of as the ideal man,

[71] *The Kingdom of God and the Son of Man* (Grand Rapids: Zondervan, 1938), p. 187.

[72] Sjøberg, *op. cit.,* pp. 97 ff.; Mowinckel, *op. cit.,* p. 355.

[73] Otto, *op. cit.,* p. 185; Mowinckel, *op. cit.,* pp. 422 ff.

[74] We cannot here discuss the Son of Man doctrine in IV Ezra, the Apocalypse of Baruch, and some of the Targums. Information is to be found in Mowinckel, *ibid.,* pp. 356 ff. and Klausner, *op. cit.,* pp. 330-65.

the pattern of what man ought to be. He is king of paradise, the ruler of the world beyond, where departed and unborn souls are. He is "the Man," by whom the universe will be restored to its original state of perfection.[75]

Something akin to this kind of thinking is to be found in the Adam speculation of Hellenistic and late esoteric Judaism. Adam was regarded as the perfect man, who stood before all other men as the prototype. At the end mankind will be redeemed by the return of Adam (the second Adam), who will restore all things to their primal state.[76]

With this background of understanding concerning the origin and meaning of the term Son of Man, we are now ready to ask one of the most vexatious questions in the whole area of New Testament interpretation: What did Jesus mean when he used it? Scholarly opinion has been sharply divided.

Vincent Taylor[77] counts some thirty-seven Son of Man sayings in the Synoptic Gospels which derive from the basic sources Q, Mark, M, and L. The term occurs thirteen times in the Gospel of John.[78] That Jesus used the term repeatedly is attested by all lines of the tradition.

Sayings concerning the Son of Man fall into three classes: (1) those having to do with Jesus present ministry (e.g., "the Son of man has nowhere to lay his head"—Luke 9:58); (2) those appearing in sayings concerning his suffering and resurrection (e.g., "how is it written of the Son of man, that he should suffer many things and be treated with contempt?"—Mark 9:12); (3) references in sayings having to do with final

[75] Mowinckel's discussion of the *Urmensch* is one of the best in recent literature (*op. cit.*, pp. 420-37). See also O. Cullmann, *op. cit.*, pp. 144 ff., and Sjøberg, *op. cit.*, Ch. IX.

[76] For a detailed exposition of this kind of thinking see Cullmann, *op. cit.*, pp. 145 ff.

[77] *The Names of Jesus*, p. 30.

[78] If the correct reading in 9:35 is "Son of Man."

events of the future (e.g., "You will not have gone through all the towns of Israel before the Son of man comes"—Matt. 10:23).

Scholarly attitudes toward the Son of Man sayings have varied widely. Rudolf Bultmann[79] disposes of categories one and two above by assuming that in category one the Hellenistic church understood the term Son of Man as a messianic designation, whereas Jesus used it only in the sense of "man" or "I," and by holding that the sayings of category two are the work of the Christian community after the passion and resurrection. He argues that when Jesus did speak of a future Son of Man (category three) he was referring to a figure other than himself. Jesus regarded himself as a prophet, a rabbi, and an exorcist, not as Messiah, suffering Servant, or Son of Man.[80]

T. W. Manson[81] some time ago advanced the view that Jesus used the term Son of Man in a collective sense, like that in Dan. 7 rather than in I Enoch, to designate the people of God, the Remnant of Isaiah, the suffering and faithful Israel, the people of God on earth who are wholly devoted to God their King. Jesus conceived his task as creating the Son of Man, the kingdom of the saints of the Most High. But the nation and even his followers gave no adequate response to God's high purpose for his people. At the end he stood alone as the Son of Man, only he "embodying in his own person the perfect human response to the regal claims of God."[82] Thus he became to the church "*the* Son of Man," and is so designated in the Gospels.

[79] *Theology of the New Testament,* I, 30.

[80] *Ibid.,* pp. 26 ff. Some American scholars who have defined Jesus' self-consciousness in prophetic terms are: Frederick C. Grant, Shirley Jackson Case, Paul E. Davies, Henry B. Sharman, Leroy Waterman, A. T. Olmstead.

[81] *The Teaching of Jesus* (Cambridge: The University Press, 1931), pp. 227 ff.

[82] *Ibid.,* p. 228.

Many scholars agree in part with Manson, finding in a few Son of Man sayings a collective meaning.[83]

George Duncan,[84] Alan Richardson,[85] and others find the background of Jesus' thought about the Son of Man principally in Ezekiel (with an assist perhaps from Daniel). To these scholars the figure of Ezekiel as God's humble, Spirit-filled messenger to the people of Israel, conscious that God had made him "a sign for the house of Israel" (Ezek. 12:6), lay before Jesus' mind. Like Ezekiel Jesus regarded himself as a God-called, Spirit-empowered, and commissioned servant. His task was to gather together the flock of God (Ezek. 34:11-16; John 10:1-18), the people to whom God would give the kingdom (Luke 12:32). Jesus saw himself as the embodiment of the true Israel, as Man as God intends man to be, as the creator of a new community of Spirit-filled brethren. Dan. 7:13 ff. may supply the background for Jesus' expectation of the triumph of the community he was creating, but the triumph he was envisaging was to be realized in history, not simply at the end of it. Jesus did not occupy his mind with speculations about an apocalyptic "coming."

Rudolph Otto [86] (and more recently Sigmund Mowinckel [87] and Oscar Cullmann [88]) has argued strongly that Jesus' views concerning the Son of Man root in part at least in the kind of thought represented in I Enoch and IV Ezra, i.e., in the

[83] Vincent Taylor (*The Names of Jesus,* p. 31) accepts this interpretation as the original meaning of the sayings in Mark 8:38 and parallels; Matt. 10:23; Luke 12:40; 17:22, 24, 26, 30.

[84] George S. Duncan, *Jesus, Son of Man* (New York: The Macmillan Co., 1949), Chs. XI-XIII.

[85] Alan Richardson, *An Introduction to the Theology of the New Testament* (New York: Harper & Brothers, 1958), pp. 128-46.

[86] *Op. cit.,* especially pp. 159-261.

[87] *Op. cit.,* pp. 445-50.

[88] *Op. cit.,* pp. 154-67.

apocalyptic eschatology of the times. I Enoch is assigned to north Palestine by Otto. He believes it was popular in some esoteric circle with which Jesus was in contact. Cullmann is of the opinion that this circle is represented by the Hellenists of the Jerusalem church, the group to which Stephen (who used "Son of Man" in referring to Jesus—Acts 7:56) belonged. Jesus may have had contact with these Hellenists during his youth and ministry.[89]

According to Otto's view and others' of like mind, Jesus believed that God had appointed him to fulfill the role of the heavenly Son of Man. But he knew also that God had called him to live and die as his suffering Servant. As "the Man" of destiny, of authority at the last Day, he went about in humility, identifying himself completely with God's lost and scattered people, opening to them through suffering service and death the kingdom of heaven. He invited men to discern who he really was, to see in him God's redemptive love, yea, even the power of the coming kingdom at work, and to believe that he would inaugurate that kingdom in glory at the last. By joining together in his consciousness the Son of Man and suffering Servant roles, he reshaped the messianic thought of Judaism so radically that the disciples had serious difficulty in understanding him. It is possible that he favored the term Son of Man because it was universalistic, rather than nationalistic, in its connotation, and because it was ambiguous (meaning both "man" and "the Man"). It presented a challenge to the hearer.[90] Thus would arise the venture of faith.

It is impossible here to evaluate these four interpretations

[89] *Op. cit.*, pp. 167 ff. On Cullmann's understanding of the place of these Hellenists in primitive Christianity see his article, "The Significance of the Qumran Texts for Research into the Beginnings of Christianity," *Journal of Biblical Literature*, LXXIV (1955), 213-26.

[90] Matthew Black, *op. cit.*, pp. 34-5; Richard Heard, *Introduction to the New Testament* (New York: Harper & Brothers, 1950), pp. 109, 121.

of the mind of Jesus.[91] It must suffice to say that most contemporary scholars feel that Bultmann is too cavalier in his handling of the data in the Gospels on the self-consciousness of Jesus and prefer to adopt one of the other three positions. That Jesus believed his role was something more than that of an eschatological prophet is widely held today. Perhaps we may say that he saw himself as God's eschatological deliverer.[92] He seems to have used the term "Son of Man" to connote both the special sovereign authority and humility in identification with men to which God had appointed him.

The fact that Jesus spoke of himself as the Son of Man deeply impressed the consciousness of his disciples and through them the tradition concerning his sayings. It is a phenomenon of no little importance that the term appears in the Gospels almost exclusively on the lips of Jesus, certainly good evidence that the tradition kept close to the mind of Jesus. That the term should appear prominently in the Fourth Gospel (thirteen times) is noteworthy. As we have seen, "Son of Man" is a Semitic term meaning "the man" or "the human being." It is properly rendered into Greek simply as "the man" (ὁ ἄνθρωπος). But the Semitic idiom is preserved in the Fourth Gospel, even though it would appear as barbarous Greek to its cultured readers.

Paul knew that the best rendering of the term would be "the man," and to give it its proper connotation as applied to Christ he wrote about "the man of heaven" (I Cor. 15:47-49. *Cf.* 15:21;

[91] See C. C. McCown, "Jesus, Son of Man, A Survey of Recent Discussion," *Journal of Religion,* XXVIII (1948), 1-12; W. G. Kümmel, *Promise and Fulfilment* (London: SCM Press, 1957); and the article by A. J. B. Higgins mentioned in note 67.

[92] Among the recent and contemporary scholars who view Jesus' self-consciousness in this way are: John Wick Bowman, Millar Burrows, Oscar Cullmann, Martin Dibelius, C. H. Dodd, Floyd V. Filson, George S. Duncan, Reginald H. Fuller, Joachim Jeremias, Werner G. Kümmel, T. W. Manson, William Manson, Chester C. McCown, Sigmund Mowinckel, Rudolph Otto, Vincent Taylor.

Rom. 5:15, 19). In both Paul and the Fourth Gospel the doctrine of the Primordial Man, known to us in Hellenism and speculative Judaism, shines through the term. For the Fourth Evangelist Jesus is the man from heaven, the archetype of humanity, the true self of the human race, who incorporates into himself the people of God that they may become what they ideally are.[93] For Paul he is the "second" or "last" Adam, through whose incarnation a new humanity, a new creation, comes into being.[94]

The Son of Man Christology clearly played a large part in the thought of the church to which the writer of the Gospel of Matthew belonged. We have noted that he uses the term thirty-one times. A study of this usage reveals several significant facts.

First, wherever the term appears in this Gospel it clearly refers to Jesus, whatever Jesus himself may have meant by it. In all of the classes of the Son of Man sayings (those concerned with Jesus' earthly ministry,[95] with his suffering and death,[96] and with his future coming[97]) the Son of Man indubitably is Jesus. In 26:2 the author inserts into the Marcan outline a prediction by Jesus of his death which Mark does not have. In 12:40 he sees a parallel to Jonah's three-day captivity in the belly of the whale in the three-day entombment of the Son of Man (Jesus) in the heart of the earth. That it is Jesus who is to return as the Son of Man is made clear by the insertion of the words "of your coming" into the Marcan query of the disciples about the sign concerning the destruction of the temple (Mark 13:4; Matt. 24:3). It is obvious from the

[93] C. H. Dodd, *The Interpretation of the Fourth Gospel*, pp. 241-49.
[94] Oscar Cullmann, *op. cit.*, pp. 169-86.
[95] E.g., Matt. 8:20; 9:6; 11:19; 12:8.
[96] E.g., Matt. 17:9, 12, 22.
[97] E.g., Matt. 10:23; 16:27, 28; 24:30, 44; 25:31.

phrase "blessed of my Father" (Matt. 25:34), a favorite form of reference to God by Jesus in the Gospel of Matthew,[98] that the Son of Man, who is also "King" (25:34, 40), is Jesus.

Secondly, for Matthew, as for the other Synoptists and the early church as a whole, it was necessary for the Son of Man to suffer in order to enter into his glory. Unmistakable traces of the doctrine of the suffering Servant of the book of Isaiah appear throughout the Gospel of Matthew. Only once, however, is the term "Servant" (παῖς) applied to Jesus (12:18), and this indirectly, by way of a quotation of Isa. 42:1-4. This one reference is more important, however, than appears on the surface, for there are only four other passages in the entire New Testament where Jesus is designated by the title "Servant" (Acts 3:13, 26; 4:27, 30). This reference offers, therefore, a clear clue concerning Matthew's Christological views.

Ernst Lohmeyer[99] has shown that the Servant conception underlies Matthew's birth and infancy narratives, several titles he uses for Jesus (Emmanuel, Nazarene, King of the Jews), the healing narratives (especially that of the paralytic in Matt. 9:1-8), some of the teaching of Jesus, and the Passion story. He believes that Matthew has kept more truly the spirit and content of the Servant point of view than any other early Christian writer.[100]

E. J. Goodspeed[101] has recently printed together Matthew's quotations from Isaiah, fifteen in number. They offer impressive evidence that our author was steeped in the language and theology of this Old Testament book.

What are some of the notes struck in Matthew's interpreta-

[98] See pp. 58 ff.

[99] *Gottesknecht und Davidssohn* (2. *Aufl.;* Göttingen, 1953).

[100] *Ibid.*, p. 46.

[101] *Matthew—Apostle and Evangelist* (Philadelphia: John C. Winston Co., 1959), pp. viii-ix.

tion of Jesus as the Servant of the Lord? (1) There is the hiddenness of the activity of the Servant. Jesus' command to silence ("he healed them all, and ordered them not to make him known"—Matt. 12:16) is explained by Isa. 42:1-4, where it is said that the Servant "will not wrangle or cry aloud, nor will any one hear his voice in the streets." (2) The Servant is endowed with the Spirit (Matt. 12:18; Isa. 42:1). Matthew, in common with the other Gospels, contains the story of Jesus' reception of the Spirit at the baptism by John the Baptist (3:16). He also explains Jesus' birth as the result of the Holy Spirit's activity (1:18 ff.). (3) The Servant ministers to the poor, the broken, the oppressed (Matt. 12:20; Isa. 42:3). He takes infirmities and bears diseases (Matt. 8:17; Isa. 53:4). He is the merciful Shepherd of the harassed and helpless (Matt. 9:36), who himself is "gentle and lowly in heart" (11:30) and inseparably identified with the least and most unfortunate of men (25:31-46). (4) He is the Savior of men from sin. His name is "Jesus, for he will save his people from their sins" (1:21). Here alone in the New Testament is the name Jesus explained. As the Servant of the Lord, a man among men commissioned by God for a special task, he forgives sins (9:1-8).[102] As the Servant he pours out his blood "for many" (*cf.* Isa. 53:12), "for the forgiveness of sins" (26:28). (5) He is the hope of the Gentiles (12:21; Isa. 42:4 in LXX). He will "proclaim justice to the Gentiles" (12:18; Isa. 42:1). Matthew shows how heathen kings brought their homage and their tribute to Jesus (2:1 ff.), and how at the last he will serve as Judge of the nations (25:31-46). Jesus, as portrayed in the Gospel of Matthew, throughout his career is God's obedient Servant, carrying out in humility, obedience, and secrecy the will of God.

[102] Matt. 9:8 puts the basis of the healing of the paralytic in a special light. See Lohmeyer, *Gottesknecht und Davidssohn,* pp. 46 ff.

The content of the Servant concept has been caught up into the Son of Man category. Though the term "Servant" does not occur in this Gospel as a title for Jesus, it is perfectly clear that, as Lohmeyer has said, "the tradition of the Son of Man was the basin into which the differing streams of the tradition, even that of the Servant of God, emptied themselves, giving up in part their special color and direction." [103]

Third, Matthew stresses more than the other Synoptists the imminent coming of the Son of Man. He utilizes all the Marcan eschatological material (Mark 13), probably all of the eschatological sayings contained in Q, and much material from a special source. He gathers these sayings together into a great discourse (Chapters 24-25), designed to awaken the church to the reality of the imminent coming of the Son of Man and the immediacy of the Great Assize.

The nearness of his coming is especially emphasized by the word *parousia* which occurs four times in the Synoptics, all of them in Matthew. In the Hellenistic-Roman period the word was in use throughout the East as a technical term for the arrival or the visit of the king or the emperor. An Egyptian papyrus of the second century B.C. presents an interesting account of Egyptian peasants toiling night and day to get ready for the *parousia* of their king.[104] Matthew exhorts his readers to watch and be diligent lest the Son of Man's sudden coming take them unawares (24:42 ff.; 25:1 ff.).[105]

[103] *Ibid.*, p. 58.

[104] Adolf Deissmann, *Light from the Ancient East* (New York: George H. Doran Co., 1927), p. 369. On the history of the word and its usage in the New Testament see Albrecht Oepke in Gerhard Kittel (ed.), *Theologisches Wörterbuch zum Neuen Testament*, V, 856-69.

[105] André Fèuillet ("Le sens du mot Parousie dans l'Évangile de Matthieu," in Davies and Daube [eds.], *The Background of the New Testament and Its Eschatology* [Cambridge: University Press, 1956], pp. 261-80) argues that *parousia* in Matthew refers not to the final manifestation of Christ at the end of the world but to the historical judgment of the Jewish people in the coming fall of Jerusalem. He finds this meaning

Matthew sets forth more clearly than the other evangelists the purpose of the Son of Man's coming. It is first of all a coming for judgment. To Mark's saying about the Son of Man's coming in the glory of his Father with the holy angels (Mark 8:38) Matthew adds "and then shall he render unto every man according to his deeds" (Matt. 16:27). In the explanation of the parable of the Tares (only in Matthew) the Son of Man at the end of the world is represented as sending forth his angels to separate the tares from the wheat (13:41). It is affirmed that at his coming "in his glory" he will sit on his glorious throne and judge all nations (25:31 ff.).

It is also a coming for the establishment of the kingdom. Concerning those standing by, Jesus is made to say not that they will not taste of death before they see the kingdom of God come with power (Mark 9:1) but that they will not taste of death "before they see the Son of Man coming in his kingdom" (Matt. 16:28). Subsequent to the Son of Man's coming and judgment the kingdom will be opened to the righteous (25:34). These will "shine like the sun in the kingdom of their father" (13:43). The Son of Man's coming and judgment are presented as the necessary prelude to the establishment of the kingdom.

As for the manner of the Son of Man's coming, it is said that he will be seen "coming on the clouds of heaven with power and great glory," and that he will send forth his angels "with a loud trumpet call" to gather together the elect from one end of heaven to the other (24:30, 31). Mark 13:26, 27 presents a parallel to most of this. Matthew has added the reference to the trumpet and writes "on the clouds of heaven"

---

also in Jas. 5:1-11 and holds that both usages are more archaic than the Pauline. Unfortunately, the interpretation by Fèuillet of the meaning of the word in Matthew is tied up with his critical views about the priority of an Aramaic Matthew and the dubious early dating of James.

for Mark's "in clouds," apparently adhering more closely than Mark to Dan. 7:13.

Immediately preceding this passage Matthew has inserted a strange reference to "the sign of the Son of man in heaven" and the remark that all of the tribes of the earth will mourn when they see it (24:30). The sign of the Son of Man may be an allusion to the ensign which was to be set up by Jehovah as a rallying point for his dispersed people.[106] If this interpretation is adopted, the reference to the trumpet blast for the gathering of the elect (24:31) is intelligible. However, the sign may be something in the sky visible to all, perhaps a shining light surrounding the Son of Man, or, if the saying is of early Christian origin, it may possibly refer to the sign of the cross.[107] Whatever the sign is, it apparently strikes terror to the tribes of the earth, for at the sight of it they break out into wailing (*cf.* Zech. 12:10-12). Matthew's insertions, whatever their meaning, at least show that he is interested in apocalyptic details connected with the coming of the Son of Man.

Cullmann's contention that the Christology of the Synoptic evangelists is not a Son of Man but rather a Messiah Christology [108] is surely erroneous as far as Matthew is concerned. It will not do to say that Matthew simply passed on a traditional belief. The Son of Man doctrine is for him fundamental to the understanding of Jesus' position and role in the purpose of God.

Finally, we must ask how the titles Messiah, Son of God, and Son of Man are related to one another in the thought of the writer of the Gospel of Matthew and what, taken together,

[106] A. H. McNeile, *The Gospel According to St. Matthew* (London: Macmillan & Co., 1915), p. 352. See Isa. 11:12; 18:3; 49:22.

[107] See Wilhelm Bousset, *The Antichrist Legend* (London: Hutchinson and Co., 1896), pp. 232 ff.; E. Klostermann, *Das Matthäusevangelium* (Tübingen, 1927), p. 195 f.

[108] *Die Christologie des Neuen Testaments,* p. 167.

they say about the basis of Jesus' authority, as presented in the First Gospel.

Our writer was doing nothing new when he interpreted Jesus' significance by the use of several different categories. All early Christians saw Jesus as the fulfillment of the many-sided hopes of Israel as expressed in the Old Testament. Paul summarizes the early Christian attitude when he writes: "All the promises of God find their Yes in him" (II Cor. 1:20).

The dominant category in the Gospel of Matthew is unquestionably that of the Son of Man. The sheer bulk of the Son of Man references and material abundantly testifies to the weight of this category in the writer's mind. The entire book moves forward toward the judgment of the Son of Man and his assumption of universal authority. The church clearly is being warned to prepare for the final eschatological event.

The ideologies represented by each of the three titles (Messiah, Son of God, Son of Man) have many points in common. The Servant of the Lord should be included also, although this term does not appear in the Gospel of Matthew as a title for Jesus. All designate the coming eschatological deliverer and suggest differing sorts of roles for him as the executor of the final purposes of God.

"The Messiah" presents him as the coming ideal king, the scion of David, who will purge God's people of evil, reign over the nations in righteousness, and teach his subjects to obey the will of God perfectly. It is possible that vestiges of the old divine king concept clung to the term into Matthew's time. If so, it would make it easy to think of the coming deliverer in transcendent terms.

So uniquely related to the being and purpose of God was Jesus, that he could be called "the Son of God." For Matthew this meant not only an ethical but also a peculiarly intimate personal relationship to God. He was God's only Son, "God with us." He called God "my Father" in a sense in which God was not the Father of the disciples. As the Son he had unique knowledge of God and unique authority for men. Man as man could not know who he really was; only God could make him known. In his works his divine glory shone through, and the disciples at times "worshiped" him. The coming King is the Son, who is entitled to a place alongside the Father and the Holy Spirit in the realm of deity.

But he lived his life on earth in the humility and obedience of a servant, unheralded and largely unrecognized by men. He was a child of the Holy Spirit both in his begetting and endowment. He ministered to the poor and unfortunate, bearing their infirmities and diseases. His true identity and destiny were known only by the Elect. He poured out his life so that men might find forgiveness of sins. His service was symbolized in his name.

Soon this hidden Servant will be revealed as the glorious Son of Man and Judge of the world. Though crucified by evil men, he is alive and waiting in full authority to consummate the purpose of God through the universal judgment and the opening of the kingdom to the righteous.

The categories thus flow together into an effective characterization of Jesus. For Matthew they explain fully Jesus' right to lordship over men.

[3]

The Authority of Jesus in the Realm of Knowledge

Now that Jesus' basic right to exercize authority has been examined, we turn to the nature of the authority exercized, as set forth in the Gospel of Matthew.

Authority, which we have defined as inherent right and manifest capability,[1] has for its field of operation two realms: knowledge and conduct. We shall want, therefore, to examine what Jesus knew, as pictured in Matthew, and how this knowledge was related to the beliefs of men; and then we shall try to determine what norms of conduct Jesus set up and how these are related to other norms and authorities. The former task will occupy our attention in this chapter.

Men have long been intrigued by Jesus' knowledge. What was its content and from whence did it come? How authoritative is his knowledge for us? I shall never forget the shock I experienced in my student days when I heard a venerable theological professor say, "Jesus didn't know that the world was round." My reaction then was, "What nonsense! Jesus had a part in making the world, didn't he? If so, he surely would know its shape!" Many laymen today hold a similar attitude toward Jesus' knowledge.

[1] See p. 47.

While it will not be possible to discuss the problem in the large here, it may be of interest to see what the writer of the Gospel of Matthew thought of Jesus' knowledge.

The Content of Jesus' Knowledge

First, it appears that Matthew does not claim for Jesus any special knowledge in the realm of everyday fact. In 4:12 it is said that Jesus withdrew into Galilee "when he heard that John had been arrested." In 14:12-13 he appends to Mark's story of the execution of the Baptist the remarks, "And they went and told Jesus" and "Now when Jesus heard this. . . ." In 15:12 the disciples are represented as coming to Jesus and asking him if he knows that the Pharisees were offended at his remarks. These comments, implying limitation in Jesus' knowledge, have no parallels in the other Gospels and seem clearly to reflect the view of the writer of the Gospel of Matthew. Plainly for Matthew Jesus' knowledge of facts and happenings was in kind and extent like that of his fellow men.[2]

Second, Jesus is represented as frequently knowing the thoughts of men.

[2] A. H. McNeile (*The Gospel According to St. Matthew* [London: Macmillan & Co., 1915], p. 356) says that Matthew "often avoids words which imply limitation of the Lord's knowledge." On p. 113 he points to Matthew's habit of omitting questions asked by Jesus, "sometimes apparently shrinking from implying ignorance on His part." The passages he lists, where Jesus' questions are omitted are: 9:22; 14:17; 16:4, 12; 17:11, 14, 18; 18:1; 19:4; 26:18. Of these 9:22; 14:17; 17:14 and 18:1 are significant. Here Matthew does omit questions of Jesus' which might imply ignorance on his part. But is this the real reason why these questions are omitted? If one will take a synopsis and examine Matthew's treatment of nearly all of Mark's narrative material, he will see how rigorously he cuts out almost all of Mark's unnecessary detail. In each case Jesus' question is unnecessary to the essential story. Hence it is omitted, together with considerable other material. If Matthew had been really careful to omit material which reflected unfavorably on Jesus' knowledge, he hardly would have written 15:12.

All of the Synoptists in stories of conflict indicate that Jesus was able to discern the thoughts of his opponents before they were expressed. Never is it indicated exactly how Jesus knew. Thus in Matt. 12:25 (a Q passage), after Jesus had been accused by the Pharisees of casting out demons by Beelzebul, the prince of demons, we find the words, "Knowing their thoughts, he said to them. . . ." How Matthew understood the phrase "knowing their thoughts" cannot be determined from the passage. It has been held by some that the use of the Greek term for "knowing" (εἰδώς) here would suggest to Matthew independent or supernatural knowledge, but this is hardly the case.[3]

In 12:15 it is said that Jesus, knowing (γνούς) the hostility of the Pharisees, withdrew from the area. In 16:8 he is said to be aware (γνούς) that the disciples are discussing among themselves the fact that they had taken no bread. In 26:10 Jesus is represented as aware (γνούς) that the disciples are complaining about the wasted ointment. In none of these cases is it said how he knew. It is possible that Matthew may have believed that Jesus possessed superhuman knowledge, but it is nowhere postulated. He may have understood this knowledge as resting on sense perception or intuition.

Third, Matthew represents Jesus as being aware of the significance of men and movements in the contemporary scene.

[3] In the Greek the form of Matthew's phrase differs somewhat from Luke's. Both have εἰδώς (some few MSS in Matthew have ἰδών, but εἰδώς is probably original) but Matthew writes ἐνθυμήσεις and Luke διανοήματα. Matthew apparently has carried ἐνθυμήσεις over from 9:4. The word implies thought of a foolish or evil sort and coincides with Matthew's anti-Pharisaic tendencies. No help is offered by the use of οἶδα rather than γινώσκω here. Though some scholars have argued that οἶδα means properly to know by reflection as opposed to γινώσκω, to know by observation (see P. Thomson, "Know in the New Testament," *The Expositor*, ninth series, III [1925], 379-82), Matthew uses the words interchangeably. In 9:4 he writes εἰδώς but in 22:18 γνούς, where the same meaning obviously is intended.

Here Matthew is quite largely dependent on the Christian tradition and shows no great deviation from it.

He portrays Jesus as being aware of the significance of John the Baptist. He devotes a sizable section of his Gospel to Jesus' attitude toward John and to Jesus' interpretation of the contemporary scene in general (11:2-24). The crucial verses are 12-14: "From the days of John the Baptist until now the kingdom of heaven has suffered violence, and men of violence take it by force. For all the prophets and the law prophesied until John; and if you are willing to accept it, he is Elijah who is to come." The specific identification of John with Elijah at the end of this passage is peculiar to Matthew. Luke has the passage substantially but without this identification (16:16). The same identification is made by Matthew in 17:13, again without a parallel in the other Gospels. Matthew is clearly interested in having Jesus mark out John's role in the plan of God, so that there may be no confusion over the matter. John is the forerunner of the Messiah; he is not the Messiah. John himself admitted that he was not worthy to baptize Jesus (Matt. 3:14). In view of the messianic claims which were being made for the Baptist by his followers in Matthew's time,[4] it is not surprising that the latter should emphasize the inferiority of John by making clear through Jesus' express statements John's position as Elijah, the forerunner.

In regard to Jesus' knowledge of the imminence of the kingdom no particular contribution is made by Matthew over that contained in Mark and Q. In all three Jesus is shown to be keenly aware of the nearness of the kingdom. One point of interest, however, may be noted. Matthew represents both John and Jesus as making the same proclamation: "Repent, for the kingdom of heaven is at hand" (3:2; 4:17). It is evident

[4] See Martin Dibelius, *Die urchristliche Überlieferung von Johannes dem Täufer* (Göttingen, 1911), pp. 87-123.

that this particular formulation of the proclamation has resulted from Matthew's adaptation of Jesus' words as recorded in Mark 1:15 and that Matthew has retrojected them into the preaching of John. What Matthew wants to show is that John knew about and sought to prepare people for the kingdom that Jesus was to inaugurate. Matthew does not mean to indicate that the source of Jesus' knowledge of the imminence of that kingdom was John the Baptist. Both John and Jesus are thus shown to possess special knowledge about the kingdom. The source of Jesus' knowledge can thus have been thought by Matthew to be no lower than John's and perhaps higher.

In regard to Jesus' understanding of the future, there is a definite crescendo in Matthew over earlier materials. Matthew not only reproduces Mark's foretellings of the passion, but he adds an additional one (26:2). He not only includes the whole of Mark's little apocalypse (Mark 13), but he expands it with sections from Q and includes considerable material from sources available only to him. He orients the whole in one direction—toward the explanation of the course of events leading up to the coming of the Son of Man and the end of the age (24:3). He is no longer interested in the events to precede the destruction of the temple, which by his time already had taken place (22:7). The whole section culminates in a spectacular judgment scene in which the Son of Man is portrayed as sitting on the throne of his glory, meting out rewards and punishments (25:31 ff.). Neither Mark nor Q has anything like this. In addition to this extended predictive discourse, Matthew presents parables (the Tares and its explanation and the Dragnet, Ch. 13) which set forth events connected with the end of the age.

All of this indicates that Matthew believed that Jesus possessed knowledge about the future quite beyond the command of ordinary men. But he does not thereby postulate omniscience for Jesus. He was aware that others besides Jesus had revealed future events. Isaiah had predicted the Virgin Birth (1:22-23); Jeremiah had prophesied the slaughter of the innocents (2:17-18) and the buying of the potter's field for thirty pieces of silver (27:9); and Zechariah had foretold the triumphal entry (21:4-5). This was prediction of the most accurate and detailed sort. Jesus' ability to foretell the future would not necessarily lift him above the level of a prophet. That Jesus' knowledge of the future to Matthew was not absolute is shown by the presence in his Gospel of Mark's saying about the time of the coming of the Son of Man (Mark 13:32; Matt. 24:36). It is said here that not even the Son knows the day or the hour.[5]

Fourth, in delineating Jesus' knowledge of the character of God, Matthew draws heavily on the rich tradition contained in earlier Christian literature. He supplements this from special sources of his own and shapes it in accordance with his particular point of view.

A survey of the Marcan material in Matthew reveals the fact that the writer of the latter Gospel is fond of the designation "Father." Some of the evidence for this was previously

[5] The phrase "neither the Son" is absent in some Greek manuscripts but is present in the most important ones. Wescott and Hort (*The New Testament in the Original Greek* [New York: Harper & Brothers, 1882], Appendix, p. 18) say that "the documentary evidence in their favour is overwhelming." Those who favor retention of the words believe they were omitted from some MSS because early scribes found them offensive doctrinally. Mark, being less read in the early church, escaped change. Those who favor their elimination believe that they arose in Matthew through assimilation to the text of Mark. Matthew's frank admission in other passages that Jesus' knowledge was in some respects, at least, limited (4:12; 14:12-13; 15:12) may help to support the retention of the words, although it must be admitted that the knowledge here spoken of is of a different kind from that contemplated in the passages just cited. The textual problem is difficult and not much weight should be given to the phrase, therefore.

presented.[6] In view of the changes he makes in Mark's wording, it is probable that he is to be credited with similar alterations in the text of Q. One may compare such passages as Matt. 6:26 with Luke 12:24, Matt. 10:29 with Luke 12:6, and Matt. 10:32-33 with Luke 12:8-9. The word "Father" in the mouth of Jesus occurs in material peculiar to Matthew twenty-four times. The probability is high that some of the occurrences of the term in this material are due to the author's editorial activity. The modifiers "heavenly" and "who is in heaven," so frequent in Matthew, appear often in rabbinic literature from the end of the first century on.[7] It is likely that this usage played a part in the shaping of the terminology of the Gospel of Matthew.

Matthew has utilized to the full the rich Q material which portrays God as a provident and loving Being. The birds; the lilies of the field; hungering, impatient, fretful men—all are objects of his concern and will be cared for as they have need (Matt. 6:26 ff.; Luke 12:22 ff.). The disciples are assured that God's ear is constantly open to their cry; asking, seeking, knocking will bring a ready response (Matt. 7:7-8; Luke 11:9-10). God is more willing to give to his earthly children than human parents are to satisfy the wants of their offspring (Matt. 7:11; Luke 11:11). There is no limit to the Father's love. Even his enemies, the unrighteous and the unjust, are objects of his concern and care (Matt. 5:45; Luke 6:35). In addition to this Q material Matthew adds significant sayings from Mark and his peculiar source. All things are possible to him who believes and prays sincerely (Mark 11:22-25; Matt. 21:21-22). The heavenly Father knows what his children need before they ask him (Matt. 6:8). He will even answer the prayer of two who shall agree about anything they ask (Matt. 18:19).

[6] See pp. 58 ff.

[7] Strack-Billerbeck, *op. cit.*, I, 393 ff.

And the Jesus of Matthew knows God as a gracious and forgiving heavenly Father. Two parables unique to Matthew emphasize this aspect of the character of God very strongly: the Unforgiving Debtor (18:23-35) and the Laborers in the Vineyard (20:1-15). The first offers the ground for forgiveness of one's fellow Christian in church and personal differences. It is: God mercifully forgives you; therefore, you ought to forgive your brother. The second points to the great-heartedness of the heavenly Father, who rewards his children not according to merit, conditioned by opportunity, but according to grace.

But another side of the character of God is presented vividly by the Jesus of the Gospel of Matthew. He is a God of righteousness and justice. Fierce is his anger against false prophets in the church, who outwardly appear like sheep but actually are ravenous wolves (7:15). These evildoers are bad trees and will be hewn down and cast into the fire of God's judgment (7:16 ff.). These persons seem to be referred to in the interpretation of the parable of the Tares (13:36-43). They will be gathered out of the Son of Man's kingdom by the angels and cast into the furnace of fire, where "men will weep and gnash their teeth." By no means all who have been brought into the Christian circle will feast with the Messiah in his kingdom. Some, who have not occupied themselves with good works, will find themselves like a guest in improper garb at a wedding feast for the king's son; they will be cast into outer darkness by the wrathful king (22:11-13). And particularly fierce is God's anger against the Jews who have rejected his plan and resisted his overtures. The wicked husbandmen will be put to a miserable death and the vineyard will be let out to other tenants (21:41). The wrath of the King will break forth upon the impudent and bloody nation; the inhabitants of Jerusalem will be destroyed and the city burned (22:7). Though God may be merciful and forgiving, he is by no means indulgent and indifferent to evil.

Fifth, Jesus' knowledge of the will of God is highlighted in the Gospel of Matthew. Inasmuch as this will be treated at length later,[8] only brief reference will be made to it here.

What does God require of man, according to the Jesus of the Gospel of Matthew? At two places in this Gospel the writer brings us up sharply, much as the author of the book of Hebrews does, when he says: "Now the point in what we are saying is this" (8:1). The first of these is 7:12, where Matthew inserts editorially, "for this is the law and the prophets." The second is 22:40, where he adds, "On these two commandments depend all the law and the prophets." The two commandments are, of course, love of God and neighbor. In 7:12 the so-called Golden Rule is said to comprise the heart of the law and the prophets.

The same emphasis on love as the heart of God's requirements appears in 19:19. Here Matthew drops from Mark's list of commandments which the inquirer about eternal life should keep, "Do not defraud," and adds, as a compensation for it, the more significant requirement, "You shall love your neighbor as yourself." It is to be noted that this commandment to love does not appear in the position occupied by Mark's "Do not defraud," but it comes at the end of the series and forms a sort of climax to the whole.

God's requirements are primarily moral and spiritual, not ceremonial, the Jesus of the Gospel of Matthew points out. God really wants justice, mercy, and faith (23:23). Matthew twice inserts into Marcan stories a quotation from Hosea which emphasizes God's true requirement: "I desire mercy, and not sacrifice" (9:13; 12:7). God wants inner, not outer, righteousness—the righteousness that exceeds that of the scribes and

[8] See Ch. IV.

Pharisees (5:20). If the inner man, the heart, is good, good works will follow (Chs. 5-7) and the Son of Man will approve these works at the last judgment (16:27; 25:31-46). What does God require? A loving and merciful heart, expressing itself in good deeds, says the Jesus of Matthew.

Sixth, Jesus is presented in the Gospel of Matthew as having clear knowledge concerning himself—who he is, what he is now doing, and what he will do.

The Jesus of this Gospel knows himself to be the Messiah, the Son of God, and the Son of Man, who now suffers but will soon come in glory. In 16:16 ff., to Peter's confession, "You are the Christ, the Son of the living God," Matthew adds an unqualified acceptance by Jesus of the designations and represents him as delighting in Peter's confession of this great truth. As we have seen, Jesus knows God as, in a unique sense, his Father. The Father reveals his secrets to his Son (11:27 ff.). Jesus regards himself as the fulfiller of the law and the prophets (5:17), as authoritative religious teacher, in fact, the second Moses,[9] whose commands are to be taught to all nations (28:19). He is aware that by his death "forgiveness of sins" will result (26:28). He knows that he is soon to come as the heavenly Son of Man, to establish his kingdom (16:28) and that he will then "sit on his glorious throne" (25:31 ff.). He represents himself as the bridegroom upon whose coming the feast in the kingdom is to be set, the prepared admitted, and the unprepared excluded (25:1-13). As King (25:34) he is also universal Judge, who will "repay every man for what he has done" (16:27. *Cf.* 25:31 ff.).

The Source of Jesus' Knowledge

In Matt. 13:54 the people of Nazareth ask, "Where did this man get this wisdom . . .?" The writer of this Gospel does not

[9] See pp. 124 ff.

there answer this question, but from 11:27 and scattered indications much can be inferred.

Jesus' knowledge in the realm of everyday fact in character and range seems to be represented as ordinary human knowledge. Jesus asks questions and is informed as human beings in general are.

There is no clear indication that Matthew attributes Jesus' knowledge of the thoughts of men to a source higher than that available to a prophet. Matthew was very familiar with the Old Testament and would know that superior knowledge is there credited to prophets. Elisha is said to know the Syrian king's words when he is in his bedchamber (II Kings 6:12). Exactly how Matthew would have explained Jesus' knowledge in this area cannot be determined.

In regard to Jesus' knowledge of the contemporary scene and of future events, it is clear that Jesus is credited with special divine illumination. Though Matthew knows of the predictive capabilities of prophets, it is obvious that he does not regard Jesus simply as a prophet. He says that the people took Jesus for a prophet (21:46), but he regards this as a superficial judgment.[10] As we have seen, Matthew regards Jesus as the divine Messiah, the heavenly Son of Man, now appearing as a man among men but soon to be revealed in glory. Matthew is aware that John the Baptist, a prophet, saw in part the significance of the times and understood something of the role of Jesus and the imminence of the kingdom, but he sees only as a way-preparer, a forerunner. He does not stand in intimate relation to the Father as does Jesus, the Son. To the Son the Father has revealed "all things" (11:27).

Jesus' knowledge of the character of God, the will of God, and of his own person and work are obviously grounded by Matthew in his status as Son of God. He is mankind's final and

[10] See p. 101.

authoritative teacher because, as the Son, he has exclusive knowledge of the Father. Therefore he can say, "Take my yoke upon you, and learn from me" (11:29). Thus he can command his disciples to "make disciples of all nations" and teach them "to observe all that I have commanded you" (28:19-20). He alone knows what God wants of men and what his final purposes for the world are.

Matthew's view of Jesus' knowledge is considerably illuminated by a consideration of beliefs concerning the Messiah and the Son of Man in Judaism. In the Psalms of Solomon it is said of the Messiah:[11] "he (shall be) a righteous king, taught of God" (17:34); "he will bless the people of the Lord with wisdom and gladness" (17:40); "his words (shall be) more refined than costly gold, the choicest . . . his words (shall be) like the words of the holy ones in the midst of sanctified peoples" (17:48-49). In I Enoch 49:1 ff. it is said of the Elect One:

> For wisdom is poured out like water,
> And glory faileth not before him for evermore.
> For he is mighty in all the secrets of righteousness,
> . . . .
> And in him dwells the spirit of wisdom,
> And the spirit which gives insight,
> And the spirit of understanding and of might,
> . . . .
> And he shall judge the secret things,
> And none shall be able to utter a lying word before him.

and in 51:3:

> And the Elect One shall in those days sit on My throne,

[11] The quotations here given of passages from the Psalms of Solomon and I Enoch are from R. H. Charles, *The Apocrypha and Pseudepigrapha of the Old Testament*, II, *ad loc.*

And his mouth shall pour forth all the secrets of wisdom
and counsel:
For the Lord of Spirits hath given (them) to him and
hath glorified him.

In the Dead Sea Scrolls great wisdom is attributed to the Teacher of Righteousness. It is said that God has made known to him all the mysteries of his servants the prophets and that what the Teacher has spoken he has received from the mouth of God.[12] Some scholars believe that the sect held that their Teacher would return as the Messiah (or one of the Messiahs), but Millar Burrows has shown how uncertain this conclusion is.[13] We cannot say, therefore, that the Qumran sectarians believed that a messianic figure would possess great wisdom, though they did postulate this of their Teacher. In the rabbinic literature, however, it is said that the Messiah will open up the riches of the Torah to the people, and that he will disclose the secret things which have lain hidden in it, the explanation of which was denied to earlier generations.[14] It is evident that persons of the first century who were acquainted with such ideas about the wisdom of the Messiah would require no answer to the question raised by the men of Nazareth, "Where did this man get this wisdom?"—provided, of course, they ascribed to Jesus this dignity.

When was the Son's unique knowledge given to him by the Father? Some scholars have held that the aorist tense of the Greek word translated "delivered" in Matt. 11:27 suggests a pre-temporal act of God, that the Son was given this knowledge

[12] 1QpHab VII. 3; II. 2.

[13] *More Light on the Dead Sea Scrolls* (New York: The Viking Press, 1958), Ch. XXVIII.

[14] Strack-Billerbeck, *op, cit.*, IV, 3. See also W. D. Davies, *Torah in the Messianic Age and/or the Age to Come* (Philadelphia: Society of Biblical Literature, 1952), Ch. IV.

in his pre-existent state. Others object to this on the ground that the aorist cannot be pressed thus, that it may refer equally well to an historical act in time. The objection is a valid one.[15] That Matthew may have believed in the pre-existence of the Messiah is quite possible. Paul obviously believed it (Phil. 2:5-11; II Cor. 8:9; I Cor. 8:6). It is plainly set forth in the Gospel of John (1:1 ff.; 8:58; 17:5). I Enoch makes explicit reference to it (48:3, 6). But we must not read the doctrine into the Gospel of Matthew on evidence as flimsy as the appearance of an aorist tense. Knowledge of the Father was given the Son at some time in the past—this the passage plainly says—but beyond this it does not go, and it is foolish to speculate concerning what Matthew may have believed about the subject.[16]

Our survey of the content and source of Jesus' knowledge, as presented in Matthew, has made possible three conclusions. First, Jesus is not regarded in this Gospel as omniscient. In the realm of outward, everyday facts his knowledge is represented as like that of other men. Second, Jesus' knowledge in the realm of religious truth is considered to have its ground in his status as Messiah-Son of Man-Son of God. Third, this knowledge was given to him by his Father. But even in this realm, if the "not even the Son" of 24:36 is an original part of the text, the Son's knowledge is not held to be absolute. Only God knows all, and he imparts what he will to the Son.

[15] See James H. Moulton, *A Grammar of New Testament Greek* (Edinburgh: T. & T. Clark, 1906), I, 140.

[16] Two other passages in Matthew may be pointed out as relevant here: 3:13 ff. and 28:18 ff. Matthew's form of the story of the baptism hardly indicates that he believed Jesus received his authoritative knowledge at that time. Here the Father is represented as chiefly concerned to certify Jesus' sonship to those around, not to impart something to Jesus. In 28:18 ff. the investiture with universal authority follows upon the resurrection and exaltation. This cannot have been regarded by Matthew as the moment when Jesus' authoritative knowledge, disclosed in his historical teaching, was received.

The Relation of Jesus' Knowledge to the Beliefs of Men

Matthew tells us that God revealed himself to his Son, both his character and his purpose for man. The Son saw and understood his own mission and destiny in the light of his understanding of the character and purpose of the Father. We have now to inquire how Matthew conceived the relation of Jesus' authoritative religious knowledge to the beliefs of the people who came into contact with him.

First, what impression did Jesus make on the religious leaders, according to Matthew? To what extent, if any, was his knowledge authoritative for them?

Throughout the Gospel of Matthew Jesus is shown in open and indeed fierce conflict with the scribes and Pharisees. The chief priests were drawn into the struggle only at the end of Jesus' ministry. Matthew reproduces Mark's stories of the disputes with the scribes and Pharisees and touches them up, adding polemical material here and there. In Matt. 9: 33-34 (a Q passage) the verdict of the Pharisees, "He casts out demons by the prince of demons," is made by Matthew to look blacker by means of contrast. He has the multitude say, "Never was anything like this seen in Israel." The same darkening by means of contrast appears in 12: 23-24, where Matthew repeats the Q account of the blind and dumb demoniac and records the widely divergent responses of the Pharisees and the crowd. In 15: 12 Matthew represents the disciples as telling Jesus that he had offended the Pharisees in his remarks about the real defilement. To this Jesus replies, "Every plant which my heavenly Father has not planted will be rooted up," which means either that the Pharisees themselves will be rooted up (and burned? *Cf.* the parable of the Tares, 13: 24 ff.), or that their teaching is a plant not planted by the Father and will be destroyed. Matthew follows this with a Q saying in which he represents Jesus as declaring plainly that the Pharisees are blind guides. Here he has changed the Q saying from a question —"Can a blind man lead a blind man? Will they not both fall into a pit?"—to a declaration,[17] thus making Jesus' attitude toward the Pharisees explicit. In Matt. 19:3 and 22:35 it is indicated (only in Matthew) that the Pharisees sought to "test" Jesus. Matthew means to indicate that they did not want to learn from him but to trip him up. It is significant that Matthew omits the response to Jesus' summary of the law made by the sincere scribe, as recorded in Mark 12:32-33. This apparently was too much for Matthew, who could conceive of no good coming from the mouth of a Pharisee. Matthew has Jesus completely vanquish the Pharisees in the debates of the last days and excoriate them roundly in the seven woes of Chapter 23.

Matthew indicates how the religious leaders felt about Jesus by the way he represents them as addressing him. To them he is only "teacher."[18] Never in this Gospel do the disciples call Jesus "teacher," even though Mark puts the term on their lips four times. This Matthew felt was appropriate for the Pharisees and those outside who knew not who Jesus was, but to the disciples he is always "Lord."[19] The final verdict of the religious leaders on Jesus is that he is an "imposter" or "deceiver" (27:63), and they request that the tomb be sealed lest "the

[17] Luke's interrogative form (6:39), says A. H. McNeile (*op. cit.*, p. 228), "is characteristic of the Lord's utterances." We find the same change from question to declaration in Matt. 16:3 (contrast Luke 12:56). The declarative form is found in Matthew also at 23:24, 26.

[18] Besides the instances given in Mark 12:14, 19, where they call him "teacher" (διδάσκαλος), which Matthew reproduces in 22:16, 24, Matthew puts this form of address on their lips (where Mark does not have it) also in 9:11. Twice in Q passages (Matt. 8:19 and 12:38) he seems to be responsible for the term, and in 22:36 a Pharisee is represented once more as addressing him thus. In this latter case the word may have been suggested to him by its occurrence in Q.

[19] Matt. 8:25; 14:28, 30; 16:22; 17:4; 18:21. "Lord" (κύριος) in Matthew implies a high degree of respect and veneration for the one thus addressed.

last fraud . . . be worse than the first." According to Matthew the religious leaders saw in Jesus only a false teacher.

Secondly, we consider the relation of Jesus' knowledge to the beliefs of the multitudes.

All of the Synoptists repeatedly record the reaction of the crowds to Jesus' teaching and works. However, Matthew particularly develops this emphasis. He not only notes the fact that the crowds did marvel over something that Jesus said or did, but he records what they said. In a Q passage (Matt. 9:33; Luke 11:14) he adds to "and the crowds marveled" the words, "Never was anything like this seen in Israel." When he repeats the same Q notice about their amazement (12:23), he adds what they said, "Can this be the Son of David?" Most often he records astonishment on their part in connection with Jesus' miracles. For this he often finds a precedent in his sources. However, as in 15:31, where he thinks some comment on the part of the crowd appropriate, he adds one on his own account. In 22:33, after Jesus' astute handling of the question about the resurrection, he writes independently, "And when the crowd heard it, they were astonished at his teaching."

That the crowd never understood Jesus, Matthew takes pains to show. Their estimate of him was superficial. To Mark's "And he entered Jerusalem" (11:11) he adds, "all the city was stirred, saying, 'Who is this?' And the crowds said, 'This is the prophet Jesus from Nazareth of Galilee'" (Matt. 21:10-11). In 21:46 Matthew forsakes Mark and writes that the authorities feared the multitudes "because they held him to be a prophet." Once Matthew has them query, "Can this be the Son of David?" (12:23). However, they never come to a clear understanding of his teaching or to an adequate recognition of his person or significance.

The reason for this lack of understanding on the part of the multitudes is given by Matthew in Chapter 13. The Scriptures had predicted that this dull-hearted people would turn a deaf ear to the divine invitation. This had come to pass. Only the Elect were able to receive the divine "secrets" set forth by Jesus. God had given to them the capacity to receive the truth, but to the multitudes this capacity had not been given (13:11). He who has this God-given capacity will be able to receive more truth, but he who has it not cannot learn new truth; he will in fact lose even such knowledge of it as he has (13:12). For Matthew Jesus' teaching resulted only in increasing misunderstanding and bewilderment on the part of the multitudes. He shrinks from Mark's statement (4:12) that Jesus intended that they should not understand (ἵνα, "in order that"), and by writing "because" (ὅτι) for Mark's "in order that" he seems to wish to show rather that they failed to understand Jesus' enigmatic teaching *because* of their hardness of heart.

This dark teaching, on the other hand, was understood by the disciples, at least in part (13:16). They had the capacity for understanding it completely when it was explained to them (13:36 ff.). Their eyes were open (13:16); the people's eyes were closed (13:15). Since this was the case with the people, they could not and did not perceive who Jesus really was. His wisdom and works amazed them, but it effected in them no wondering confession of faith like that made by the disciples, "Truly you are the Son of God" (14:33) or that by Peter, "You are the Christ, the Son of the living God" (16:16). Jesus' distinctive knowledge was in no real way communicated to them. They could not receive it. To them he was only a prophet.

Thirdly, Matthew delineates at length the relation of Jesus' knowledge to the beliefs of the disciples.

Mark frequently states that the disciples failed to understand sayings of Jesus, that their hearts were hardened, that they had eyes but saw not. To the very end of Mark's Gospel the disciples cannot grasp who Jesus is and what his mission in life is. In Matthew all this is changed. The disciples do comprehend Jesus' real identity and what he is trying to tell them.

They do not understand everything fully, to be sure, but they show real flashes of insight, and have thoroughly receptive minds. Let us look at the evidence for this.

The alterations in favor of the disciples begin in Matt. 13. In Mark 4:10 it is said that the disciples ask Jesus concerning the parables, i.e., about their meaning. That this is what they have in mind is shown in Mark 4:13 by Jesus' reply, "Do you not understand this parable? How then will you understand all the parables?" Matthew, on the other hand, has the disciples ask, "Why do you speak to them in parables?" (13:10), and he omits the rebuke given in Mark 4:13. To the disciples it is given to know the secrets of the kingdom of heaven (Matt. 13:11). They possess some knowledge already. More will be given to them (Matt. 13:12). That their eyes are open and that they do see and understand, Matthew shows in the form he gives to the Q saying in Matt. 13:16-17. In Luke's version (10:23-24), which is certainly more original, the emphasis is on the things which the disciples see, the signs of the dawning kingdom apparently: "Blessed are the eyes which see what you see!" Matthew has, "But blessed are your eyes, for they see, and your ears, for they hear." Now when Matthew comes to the explanation of the parable of the Sower, Mark's rebuke of the disciples for not understanding, would, of course, be out of place and misleading. Hence he omits it and writes only, "Hear then the parable of the sower" (Matt. 13:18). Jesus is represented in Matthew as giving the explanation to the disciples as a matter of course. They possess the spiritual capacity to receive and understand the truth. He explains to them also the parable of the Tares and the parable of the Dragnet, and when he is through with all the parables he asks, "Have you understood all this?" and they answer "Yes" (Matt. 13:51). How different this is from Mark's picture of the disciples will become increasingly apparent.

Matthew's statement in 14:33 concerning the disciples' reaction to Jesus' walking on the water is vastly different from that offered in the parallel passage in Mark (6:51-52). Mark has, "And they were utterly astounded, for they did not understand about the loaves, but their hearts were hardened." Matthew writes, "And those in the boat worshiped him, saying, 'Truly you are the Son of God.'" The difference here speaks for itself.[20]

The way is now prepared for Peter's great confession (Matt. 16:16): "You are the Christ, the Son of the living God." This is shown in Matthew to be no at-the-moment, unfounded leap of faith. It is the natural result of the disciples' seeing eyes and hearing ears. Jesus had been teaching them the secrets of the kingdom of heaven and about the Son of Man who was to inaugurate that kingdom (Ch. 13). He had opened to them the rich stores of his knowledge. They had understood all that he had said to them (13:51). Their formal confessions (14:33; 16:16) thus epitomize what they have learned, and the teacher commends the comprehension of his chief disciple (16:17 ff.).

In Matt. 16:8 ff. another striking alteration of Mark (8:17 ff.) is to be seen. Here Mark records Jesus as saying to the disciples, "Why do you discuss the fact that you have no bread? Do you not yet preceive or understand? Are your hearts hardened? Having eyes do you not see, and having ears do you not hear? And do you not remember?" Then he asks them about the baskets left over from the feeding of the five thousand and the seven thousand, and he concludes with the question, "Do you not yet understand?" (8:21). Matthew takes large liberties with this passage. He begins Jesus' words with "O men of

[20] The attempt of Ned B. Stonehouse (*The Witness of Matthew and Mark to Christ* [2nd ed.; Grand Rapids, Mich.: Wm. B. Eerdmans Publishing Co., 1958], pp. 218 ff.) to harmonize the two points of view is hardly successful because it considers the passages in isolation from the other data of both Gospels in which the representation of the disciples' understanding is to be seen.

little faith . . ." They have faith but not enough! He includes Mark's "Do you not yet perceive . . . ?" but omits "or understand? Are your hearts hardened? Having eyes do you not see, and having ears do you not hear?" This apparently sounded too much like Isaiah's "prophecy" which he already had applied to the multitudes, to whom it was not given to know the secrets of the kingdom of heaven (13:11). The disciples' eyes saw; their ears heard (13:16). How then could it be said of them that their hearts were hardened and that they saw not and heard not? Hence, he cuts all of this out, and at the end of the section, in place of Jesus' "Do you not yet understand?" he writes, "Then they understood that he did not tell them to beware of the leaven of bread, but of the teaching of the Pharisees and Sadducees" (16:12). The trouble with the disciples was that they had "little faith" (16:8).

In Mark 9:10 it is suggested strongly that the disciples failed to understand what Jesus meant by his reference to the rising of the Son of Man from the dead. This entire verse is omitted by Matthew, although Jesus' command regarding secrecy, just preceding in Mark, is given in full. In the discussion concerning Elijah (Mark 9:11-13; Matt. 17:10-13) Matthew takes pains to add to Jesus' enigmatic words about Elijah's having come already the fact that Jesus succeeded in communicating to his disciples his knowledge concerning the significance of John: "Then the disciples understood that he was speaking to them of John the Baptist" (Matt. 17:13).

After the second prediction of the passion of Jesus, Mark adds, "But they did not understand the saying, and they were afraid to ask him" (9:32). In place of Mark's unfavorable picture of the disciples Matthew writes, "And they were greatly distressed" (17:23). It is obviously suggested that they grasped what he meant or they would not have been distressed over the announcement. In the third prediction Mark's "and they were amazed, and those who followed were afraid" (10:32) is omitted by Matthew. Luke got the point of Mark's account. He adds quite independently, "But they understood none of these things; this saying was hid from them, and they did not grasp what was said" (18:34).

Now, what significance have all of these changes for our understanding of Matthew's attitude toward the relation of Jesus' knowledge to the thought and beliefs of the disciples? Many commentators see in these changes only a desire on the part of Matthew to eliminate from the gospel story everything which put the pillars of the Christian church in an unfavorable light.[21] They point to similar attempts by Matthew to eliminate from Mark's picture of Jesus unfavorable elements, and are content to let the matter rest there. Some, like Pierson Parker, who believe in the priority of the Gospel of Matthew (or an earlier form of that Gospel),[22] hold that Mark, rather than Matthew, has done the changing. They argue that the Gospel of Mark reflects the Judaizing controversy in the church and the Gentile-Christian attempt to play down the authority of the first "Jewish" disciples. Mark wished to disparage the Jewish-Christian position which is associated in the Gospel of Matthew with these disciples.[23] We have seen reason for doubting the priority of Matthew, and without this conclusion the explanation falls to the ground.

A number of facts indicate that a better explanation can be given. It is important to note that Matthew not only points out that the disciples understood Jesus' teaching but he insists that *every* hearer of the gospel message must *understand* it, if he is to become a disciple.

In the explanation of the parable of the Sower (Matt. 13:

[21] For example, in the commentaries on Matthew of Willoughby C. Allen, A. H. McNeile, Alfred Plummer, Nathaniel Micklem.

[22] See pp. 20 ff.

[23] Pierson Parker, *op. cit.*, pp. 104 ff.

18 ff.), Matthew writes: "When any one hears the word of the kingdom and does not understand it, the evil one comes and snatches away what is sown in his heart." At the end of the explanation Matthew has, "As for what was sown on good soil, this is he who hears the word and understands it; he indeed bears fruit . . ." (13:23). Mark has neither of these references to understanding. Clearly, for Matthew, it is necessary not only to hear but also to understand the message about the kingdom in order to become and remain a true disciple. Understanding is for him a prerequisite and a requisite for salvation. The multitudes did not have the capacity for understanding the secrets of the kingdom of heaven; the disciples did; and anyone who becomes a genuine disciple likewise will understand.

What are the secrets that must be understood? Matthew sets them forth in part in his parable chapter (Ch. 13); but the whole Gospel must be drawn on for an answer.

Disciples must understand that God has a heavenly kingdom which he proposes to set up at the end of the age. Its value for man is to be compared to that of a hidden treasure or a costly pearl (13:44-45). They must understand Jesus' relation to this coming kingdom: who he really is, what he is doing in the world, and what he will do in the future. Like Peter and the other disciples they must know that Jesus is the Messiah, the Son of the living God (14:33; 16:16), the coming Son of Man, who will admit and exclude from the heavenly kingdom (13:37-43; 25:31-46). They must understand that the Son of Man during his earthly ministry is sowing the seed of the kingdom in the world, thereby raising up sons for the kingdom (13:37 ff.); that the Son of Man must take the path of suffering and death in order to effect "forgiveness of sins" (26:28); and that he expects his disciples to follow in his footsteps (10:24-42; 16:24 ff.). They must understand the basis upon which final destiny will be determined. The doers of evil (7:23; 13:41), those who cause others to stumble and fall into sin (13:41; 18:6 ff.; 24:11), those not clothed in the garment of good works (22:11-13), the indifferent to the suffering and needy (25:31-46), those who exalt the lesser commands of the law above the command to love of God and neighbor and thus are outwardly correct but inwardly corrupt (Ch. 23)—all will be gathered up and cast "into the furnace of fire" where "men will weep and gnash their teeth" (13:42). But the inwardly righteous and outwardly merciful and benevolent, the true sons of the Father, will inherit the kingdom prepared for them from the foundation of the world (25:34). They must watch and wait for their coming Lord (25:1-13), giving diligence in the interim to be morally and spiritually prepared (24:42-51).

It is now apparent why Matthew changed Mark's picture of the disciples where their comprehension of Jesus' teaching was involved. He held that God had revealed in and through Jesus his purposes for the world. He believed that it was by hearing and understanding this revelation that one would attach himself to Jesus and prepare himself spiritually and morally for the end of the age and the advent of the kingdom of heaven. The Gospel of Matthew as a whole is simply a commentary on the crucially important passage 11:27-30. The Father has revealed his secrets to the Son. The Son in turn reveals them to his disciples. He thus invites men to come and learn from him, and if they do, they will find rest for their souls. The Son is the world's teacher and savior (28:18-20). Upon their comprehension of his teaching their salvation rests.

Jesus thus appears in the Gospel of Matthew as the world's hierophant. Possessing knowledge of the secrets of God, he reveals them to his disciples. They, in turn, reveal them to others. They are thus lights in the world and, like their esteemed Master, also hierophants of the divine revelation. Therefore, Jesus enjoins them to "make disciples of all nations" and to teach the converts to observe all that he has commanded (28:19-20).

We shall leave to Chapter V consideration of the reasons for Matthew's strong emphasis on revelation and understanding and turn now from *knowing* to *doing,* as presented in this Gospel.

[4]

The Authority of Jesus in the Realm of Conduct

THE problem of authority was the most perplexing and pressing problem the church faced in the Apostolic Age. Since the appearance of Jesus, a circle with one focus—the law of Moses—had become an ellipse with two foci: the words of Moses and the words of Jesus.

What was the relationship between the revelation in Moses and the revelation in Jesus? Was the will of God for the life of the church expressed both in Moses and in Jesus, or only in Jesus? If the church was Israel as God intended it to be, the true Israel, could it ignore the basis of its life as the people of God: the covenant at Sinai? Or was there some way in which it could offer loyalty both to the lawgiver of mount Sinai and the Messiah of the mount of Beatitudes and mount Calvary?

The Gospel of Matthew grapples with this problem. The answer it proposes obviously was a masterful one, at least to the mind of the early church, for the Gospel of Matthew speedily became the church's favorite Gospel.

Jesus' Attitude Toward the Oral Tradition of the Pharisees

In this Gospel Jesus is almost everywhere represented as in mortal conflict with the Pharisees. They try to catch him up, and he in turn seeks to confound them. He criticizes them chiefly on two grounds.

In the first place, their righteousness is external. It consists of acts and ceremonies; it is not of the heart. One thinks immediately of Jesus' strictures against practicing one's piety before men, such as blowing a trumpet before giving alms, standing in public places when praying, and speaking in flowery language to impress God or, rather, one's auditors (6:1-18). One thinks also of the charge that the Pharisees tithe "mint and dill and cummin" but neglect "the weightier matters of the law, justice and mercy and faith" (23:23). They are called "hypocrites" who "preach, but do not practice" (23:3). They are said to be outwardly righteous but within to be "full of hypocrisy and iniquity" (23:28).

Secondly, their man-made tradition often violates the will of God. The Pharisees had attempted to bring the whole of Israel's life under the will of God as expressed in the law of Moses. But the written law was not comprehensive and detailed enough in its requirements to cover all aspects of Jewish life. R. Travers Herford has explained the situation thus:

> The Torah, as written, left the Jew at many points without specific directions, gave him no clear intimation at all, as to what the divine will was in such-and-such a case. Therefore the Torah needed an interpreter who should be able to deduce from what it did say in one case what it would say in another case if it had expressly dealt with that other case.[1]

This is precisely the problem we face in the United States when we attempt to apply a somewhat ancient Constitution to the tangled affairs of twentieth-century American life. To do this interpreting a body of experts, known as the Supreme Court, exists. The decisions of this Court, through the long years of its history, are as binding as the constitution itself. Among the

[1] *The Pharisees* (New York: The Macmillan Co., 1924), p. 71.

Jews the interpretations were made by outstanding rabbis, individually and collectively. By a kind of pious fiction the authority of Moses was claimed for these interpretations. It was said that God had given to Moses at Sinai both the written law and its oral interpretation. The latter had been handed down generation after generation orally.[2]

The importance of the oral tradition in Pharisaic teaching is expressed thus by L. Finkelstein: "The belief in the oral law, once accepted, became the cornerstone of the whole Pharisaic building; it summed up in itself all the Pharisees' teachings, doctrinal and legal." [3]

The Gospels point out clearly that Jesus clashed with the Pharisees over the authority of the oral tradition. Matthew introduces from Mark Jesus' controversy with them over hand-washing before eating (Mark 7:1 ff.; Matt. 15:1 ff.). Matthew expands Mark's record of Jesus' attack on "the tradition of men," which has been substituted for "the commandment of God" (Mark 7:8), by adding an episode. He writes that the disciples came to Jesus and told him that the Pharisees were offended at his remarks, to which Jesus replied, "Every plant which my heavenly Father has not planted will be rooted up. Let them alone; they are blind guides. And if a blind man leads a blind man, both will fall into a pit" (15:13-14). This expanded version of the altercation of Jesus with the Pharisees leaves little doubt how Matthew himself felt about the bulk, at least, of Pharisaic tradition.

But how can Matthew remark that the disciples were told by Jesus to beware of the teaching of the Pharisees (16:12) and later quote Jesus as exhorting them to "practice and observe whatever they tell you" (23:3)? The attitude toward the teach-

[2] George Foot Moore, *Judaism in the First Centuries of the Christian Era* (Cambridge: Harvard University Press, 1927), I, 251 ff.

[3] "The Pharisees: Their Origin and Their Philosophy," *Harvard Theological Review,* XXII (1929), 245.

ing of the Pharisees is obviously inconsistent here. Which really represents the attitude of Matthew?

Some scholars think that Matthew means to say that Jesus accepted Pharisaic interpretation as valid and that he attacked only the failure of the Pharisees to *practice* what they *preached*. His central charge against them is that they are "hypocrites"; he does not oppose their teaching as such. To be sure, Jesus in 15:3 ff. criticizes them for misuse of their tradition, so as to invalidate the law of God, but he does not oppose the tradition itself.[4]

One may doubt that this adequately represents Matthew's intent. In 15:13 and 16:12, both passages without parallels in the other Gospels, Matthew's attitude is sufficiently clear: the Pharisees and all they stand for are plants not planted by the heavenly Father, whose destiny is rooting up. He shows throughout his Gospel that they maliciously opposed Jesus' words and works. Their hostility was influential in bringing about Jesus' death. Because of their opposition to the purposes of God, Jesus said to them, "The kingdom of God will be taken away from you and given to a nation producing the fruits of it" (21:43, 45).

It is likely, therefore, that those scholars are right who hold

[4] Günther Bornkamm and Gerhard Barth in Bornkamm, Barth, and Held, *Überlieferung und Auslegung im Matthäusevangelium,* especially pp. 28 ff., 80 ff. Barth points out that Matthew accepts some elements of the Pharisaic tradition (cf. Matt. 5:21, 43; 12:11; 23:23) and argues that he therefore does not oppose the oral tradition on principle. But Barth sees that Matthew's conception of love as the sum and substance of the law really breaks through the whole Pharisaic tradition-structure. Now it may be granted that Matthew (or sources used by him) accepts some elements of Pharisaic tradition, but he obviously is opposed to what Pharisaism fundamentally stands for: obedience to Pharisaic *Halakoth* as a requisite for salvation (see below, pp. 135 ff.). Bornkamm and his students see Matthew and his church as not yet separated from Judaism; the struggle is still *intra muros.* As we noted in Ch. I, this point of view is open to serious question.

that in Chapter 23 Matthew has drawn on a source which is more Judaistic than he himself is. In reproducing it he was not careful to assimilate it to his own point of view.[5] It is true that Matthew admits the legitimacy and necessity of interpretation of the law—he himself does it as a scribe "trained for the kingdom of heaven" (13:52)—but he is obviously against the Pharisaic way of interpreting it. The true interpretation of the law is that given by Jesus.

Jesus' Attitude Toward the Written Law

Does Matthew anywhere represent Jesus as rejecting or overriding the commandments of the written law? The answer clearly is No. Matthew shows that Jesus attacked only the tradition of the elders and its chief exponents, the Pharisees; he in no way opposed the law of Moses itself.

Two passages are instructive here. The first, 15:10-20, has already been considered in part. Matthew's reworking of Mark's account of the controversy over the disciples' failure to wash their hands before eating (Mark 7:1-13) offers significant indications of his point of view.

In Mark the discussion shifts from the question of the tradition about the washing of hands before eating to the deeper implications. Jesus calls the people to him and tells them plainly, "There is nothing outside a man which by going into him can defile him; but the things which come out of a man are what defile him" (7:15). This logion, being in the form of a "parable" (7:17), requires explanation, which Jesus is recorded as giving. He tells them that food cannot defile a man religiously, because it goes into the stomach, not into the heart,

[5] Burnett Hillman Streeter, *The Four Gospels*, pp. 253 f.; G. D. Kilpatrick, *The Origins of the Gospel According to St. Matthew*, p. 35; Sherman E. Johnson, *The Interpreter's Bible*, VII, 528-29; Morton Smith, "The Jewish Elements in the Gospels," *Journal of Bible and Religion*, XXIV (1956), 96.

and religion is a matter of the heart. Mark, seeing the vital significance of this pronouncement, adds, "Thus he declared all foods clean" (7:19). This comment of Mark's shows that he regards the issue to be no longer washing of hands but the whole question of clean and unclean. He seems to understand Jesus to have set aside with a word the Pentateuchal food laws. He does not mention the controversy over handwashing again. This he views merely as the occasion for Jesus' new and revolutionary teaching.

Matthew definitely hedges in this section. He makes it appear that Jesus is attacking the teaching of the Pharisees, not the written law. This is evident from three considerations.

1) By his insertion of 15:12-13 he indicates that the central logion, which he gives as "Not what goes into the mouth defiles a man, but what comes out of the mouth, this defiles a man" (15:11), was directed against the teaching of the Pharisees. When Jesus is told that his dart had gone home, that the Pharisees were offended at his words, he is represented as replying that the Pharisees (or their teaching)[6] are plants not planted by the Father. The attack on the Pharisees is continued with the citation in somewhat altered form of a Q passage concerning the blind leading the blind (Matt. 15:14; Luke 6:39). By directing Jesus' attack at the Pharisees, not at the written law as in Mark, Matthew shows that the whole system of Pharisaic piety, rather than the law, was undermined by Jesus' logion.

2) By adding at the very end of the section the words "but to eat with unwashed hands does not defile a man" (15:20), Matthew plainly represents the whole of Jesus' attack, described in 15:10-20, as aimed not against the law but against

[6] Most likely the Pharisees themselves are meant, as analogous passages (Psalms of Solomon 14:3 ff.; Jubilees 1:16; Matt. 3:10, 12; 13:29; Luke 13:7) seem to show (see E. Klostermann, *Das Matthäusevangelium* [Tübingen, 1927], p. 133).

scribal tradition. For him the matter at issue all the way through is the tradition of the elders about the washing of hands.

3) Matthew omits Mark's "Thus he declared all foods clean." He wishes to avoid setting Jesus squarely against the written law, which is done by this comment of Mark's.

The second passage involving the written law is Matt. 19:3-9. In Mark's account (10:2-12) the Pharisees ask Jesus if it is lawful for a man to put away his wife *at all.* In reply Jesus states unequivocally that it was not God's intention that men should divorce their wives and that the liberty permitted by Moses (Deut. 24:1 ff.) was contrary to the divine will. Matthew has altered Jesus' position radically. The Pharisees no longer ask Jesus if it is lawful *at all,* but they ask whether it is lawful *for every cause.*[7] The right of divorce is presupposed. They merely ask him to interpret Moses. What causes did Jesus think were adequate grounds for the divorce which Moses permitted? Jesus is thus made to enter the dispute which was going on between the liberal school of Hillel, which held that a man could divorce his wife for the most trifling reasons, and the school of Shammai, which insisted that unchastity was the only legitimate ground. Jesus is made to side with the Shammaites: It is not lawful to divorce "for every cause" but it is lawful for "unchastity" (19:9). The issue in Matthew is not the rightness or wrongness of the law of Moses; the matter at stake is only the interpretation of the law. Again Matthew has eliminated the radical elements in Mark's account.

The Jesus of Matthew's Gospel does not attack the Mosaic

[7] The translation in the Revised Standard Version, "for any cause," does not carry the clear force of the Greek (κατὰ πᾶσαν αἰτίαν); it may, in fact, suggest quite the wrong meaning. Verse 9 shows conclusively that Matthew understands the issue to be whether the school of Hillel is right in permitting divorce on a multiplicity of grounds. Thus we should translate here, "for every cause."

law; rather, he positively affirms its validity. A key passage is Matt. 5:17-48.

This section begins with an affirmation by Jesus that he came not to abolish the law and the prophets but to fulfill them (5:17). This is followed by statements which emphasize the validity of the whole law and the necessity of obeying and inculcating obedience to all of its commandments (5:18-19). It is then asserted that the scribes and Pharisees, who, it is implied, do not interpret and obey the law aright and thus do not possess the higher righteousness, will not enter the kingdom of heaven (5:20). Jesus shows what the law and the prophets really require: inner goodness, integrity, and abounding love, not simply conformity in the realm of overt acts. Those who possess these qualities of the inner spirit obey the law as it was meant to be obeyed and will find entrance to the kingdom of heaven. Such is the general trend of the thought in this section.

But we must pause for closer examination of some of the statements here. How precisely does Matthew believe Jesus fulfilled the law and the prophets?

Matt. 5:17-19 is a storm center of New Testament interpretation. To what extent do these verses represent the mind of Jesus, of the primitive church, of Matthew himself? What do the key words and phrases here mean, whatever their origin? Scholars have long held the most diverse opinions on these questions. We shall attempt to discover only what the verses seemed to mean to Matthew, regardless of their origin and history.

How must he have understood the statement that Jesus came not to abolish the law and the prophets but to fulfill them (5:17)? A Swedish scholar, Henrik Ljungman, has written a whole book on this verse and a related passage (Matt. 3:15).[8]

[8] *Das Gesetz Erfüllen—Matth. 5.17 ff. und 3.15 untersucht* (Lund, 1954).

In this exhaustive study the chief positions advocated by scholars on the meaning of "fulfil" (πληρόω) are summarized. 1) It is held that the word means "to do" or "to carry out": Jesus came not to abolish the law but to carry it out by obeying it. When it is fully obeyed, then it is fulfilled. 2) To fulfill the law and the prophets is to reveal their true meaning, to give them a concise and final interpretation, to show their deepest intentions. Jesus is thus set forth in this verse as the revealer of the true will of God hidden in the wording of the law and the prophets. 3) The word means "to establish," "to validate" the law and the prophets. It stands here in opposition to the word "abolish." Jesus means to affirm the abiding validity of the word and the will of God as expressed in the Scriptures. What God has promised in the prophecies of the Scriptures he will perform.

Ljungman objects to these interpretations and proposes a fourth position, which he derives in part from study of a parallel saying in Matt. 3:15—"for thus it is fitting for us to fulfil all righteousness"—and also from the context of 5:17. He takes "righteousness" in 3:15 to mean not "acts of righteousness" or an ethical quality of goodness or uprightness but rather God's eschatological judgment of the wicked and salvation of the elect. Jesus knows that he has come to effect by his sacrificial death eschatological judgment and salvation. In his coming and through his work the will of God as expressed in the Scriptures is accomplished. The Scriptures in their totality are thus "fulfilled" by him who is their soul and center. Jesus has not come to fulfill prophecies merely, but to accomplish the redemptive purpose of God as set forth in the Scriptures. By his sacrificial self-giving the disciple is brought into right relation with God and thus possesses the exceeding righteousness mentioned in Matt. 5:20.

Is Ljungman right here? Does Matt. 5:17 mean, "I came not

to abolish the law and the prophets but rather to accomplish through my sacrificial death the purpose of God (judgment and salvation) set forth in them?"

"Fulfil" (πληρόω) occurs in Matthew sixteen times, twelve of which are in the passive voice and have to do with the fulfillment of prophecy: "This was to fulfil what the Lord had spoken by the prophet." [9] Here the word quite clearly means "carry into effect" or "bring to pass." Matthew is simply saying that such-and-such a passage of the Old Testament is no longer a promise. Certain events in the life of Jesus happened in order that the word of the Lord through the prophet might be "carried into effect" or "brought to pass." A similar usage is to be seen in Acts 3:18, where Peter says, "What God foretold by the mouth of all the prophets, that his Christ should suffer, he thus fulfilled (ἐπλήρωσεν)," that is, "carried out" or "brought to pass." The central idea is that of *realization.*

Twice the word is used in Matthew in the sense "to be full" or "to fill up" (pertaining to objects): the net (13:48) and the measure (23:32) which became full. Here the idea is simply *completion,* filling up what is lacking.

The two remaining occurrences of the word are in the crucial passages 3:15 and 5:17. Without a clear understanding of the meaning of these verses Matthew's conception of Jesus' attitude toward the law cannot be determined.

We begin with the phrase "all righteousness" (πᾶσαν δικαιοσύνην) in 3:15, which Jesus says he must "fulfil." As we have seen, Ljungman asserts that the word "righteousness" here cannot mean "acts of righteousness" or refer to an ethical quality but must be taken in an eschatological sense: the putting right of all things by the Messiah, thus his judgment of the wicked and salvation of the Elect. Oscar Cullman takes

[9] ἀναπληρόω occurs once (13:14), without apparent distinction of meaning.

the phrase to mean "a general forgiveness," which Jesus will effect by his death.[10]

Unfortunately, the other occurrences of the word "righteousness" in Matthew do not seem to bear out this alleged eschatological meaning. In 6:1 the word clearly means acts or practices of piety, which one may do in a right or wrong way. The exceeding righteousness of 5:20 is defined in the antitheses of 5:21-48. Here the thought turns about attitudes and behavior. As we shall see immediately, what God wants is inner goodness and integrity, not simply outward conformity to legalistic norms. In 21:32 John's coming "in the way of righteousness" seems to refer to his demand for attitudes and conduct in conformity with the will of God. In 5:6 "righteousness" may well be a gift from God sent now to those who long for it, and not eschatological vindication. In 6:33 the eschatological meaning is possible, though not absolutely demanded. "His righteousness" here may mean life in accordance with the divine will, which, as we shall see, is in Matthew the prerequisite for entrance to the kingdom of heaven. In no usage of the term in the passages thus far considered is a forensic-eschatological interpretation of "righteousness" required, and in several instances attitudes and behavior before God in the present are clearly embraced by the term. A presumption is therefore established that the meaning in 3:15 will conform to this general usage, unless there are strong reasons to the contrary.

In 3:15, which has no parallel in the other Gospels, we seem to be dealing with an apologetic comment, perhaps Matthew's, by which Jesus' baptism at the hands of John is explained.[11] He was not baptized because he was a sinner, as were the others, but because it was fitting and his duty to do all that

[10] *Baptism in the New Testament* (London: SCM Press, 1950), p. 18.
[11] Cf. Günther Bornkamm, *Jesus von Nazareth* (Stuttgart, 1956), p. 44.

God had declared to be his will. Surely nothing more is needed here for the content of "all righteousness" than all those attitudes and acts which accord with the divine will for men.

If this is the meaning of righteousness here, then the content of the word "fulfil" is fairly well determined. It can only mean to carry out, to perform, what God requires of man, the meaning ascribed to the word in 5:17 by one group of scholars, as we saw above. One is hardly justified in finding in the phrase in 3:15 a reference to a sacrificial death by which eschatological judgment and salvation is to be accomplished, unless the usages in Matthew clearly require such content.

We come now to 5:17 with two possible meanings of the word "fulfil" in mind, both appearing in the Gospel of Matthew: to bring to pass, to carry into effect, to realize something promised; and to carry out, to perform. Does either of these fit the context in which 5:17 appears? In the final analysis the context must be determinative here.

That Matthew may have understood fulfilling the law and the prophets to mean bringing the predictions contained in them to realization is certainly not impossible, in view of his pronounced interest in the fulfillment of prophecy. It may well be that the phrase "and the prophets" of 5:17 is an addition of Matthew's. In Matt. 26:56, "of the prophets"—a clear editorial insertion—shows his interest in this portion of the Old Testament. He is fond of the collocation law and prophets, as his comments in 7:12 and 22:40 show. He may also have added to the Q saying about the unchangeability of the law (Matt. 5:18; Luke 16:17) the phrase "until all is accomplished (γένηται)." Substantially the same phrase, translated in the Revised Standard Version "till all these things take place," appears in 24:34 (and parallels in Mark and Luke), to which saying the phrase in Matt. 5:18 may owe its origin.[12] Though other interpreta-

[12] E. Wendling, "Zu Matthäus 5,18.19," *Zeitschrift für die neutestamentliche Wissenschaft,* V (1904), 253 ff.

tions are possible, the phrase may add another bit of evidence that Matthew wished to emphasize Jesus' bringing to pass all that was predicted in the Old Testament, and that this is what he understood Jesus to mean in the saying recorded in 5:17.

The difficulty with this line of interpretation is that it makes poor connection with the material following. Verse 18 asserts the indissolubility and indivisibility of the law: the whole law, without even the tiniest exception, will have validity as long as the world lasts.[13] Because of the continuing validity of the whole law, all of its precepts must be obeyed and inculcated (vs. 19). But the law must not be obeyed after the manner of the scribes and Pharisees; it must be obeyed according to its true meaning, which Jesus alone has set forth (vss. 20-48).

Jesus' interpretation of the law is now given in a series of antitheses. What God wants is not refraining from murder only, but from the anger which prompts it; not avoidance of adultery only, but the lustful thought that lies behind it; not attention to the legalities of divorce, but abstention from divorce at all (except on the ground of infidelity); not the eschewing of false swearing, but possession of the kind of integrity which makes swearing unnecessary; not eye-for-eye and tooth-for-tooth justice, but overwhelming generosity toward abusers; not hatred of enemies, but Godlike love and concern for them.

One gathers, therefore, from the way Matthew has put his materials together in 5:17-48 that he wishes to say that Jesus asserted the full validity of the law and the prophets (i.e., the Scriptures) and that he wished to show how they should be understood and obeyed. The true righteousness is inner goodness and integrity, not adherence to regulations governing outward behavior.

That Jesus is intent on showing the true meaning of the law

[13] Ljungmann, *op. cit.,* pp. 36 ff.

and the prophets is stressed by Matthew elsewhere in his Gospel. In two important and unique passages he points out that the essence of the law and the prophets is the commandment to love: "whatever you wish that men would do to you, do so to them; for this is the law and the prophets" (7:12); and love God and love your neighbor—on these two commandments "depend all the law and the prophets" (22:40). Furthermore, Jesus is twice made by Matthew to quote Hosea when he is criticized by the Pharisees, who do not understand the Scriptures aright: "Go and learn what this means, 'I desire mercy, and not sacrifice' " (9:13; 12:7). Jesus declares that the chief commandments of the law are justice, mercy, faith; tithing and other ceremonial requirements are of secondary importance (23:23). Matthew shows that the chief commandment of the law constantly motivated Jesus to actions which were out of keeping with the standards of Pharisaic Judaism, but not out of line with the real intent of the law. On the contrary, they were the fulfillment of the law. Matthew regards Jesus as a true Jew, a Jew after God's own heart, who lived not as a rebel against the law, but who actually obeyed it by living up to its heart and essence.

In the light of all these considerations, what then did Matthew conceive Jesus to mean in the statement, "Think not that I have come to abolish the law and the prophets; I have come not to abolish them but to fulfil them"? Surely that he had come to show what they really mean, how they should be obeyed, to obey them in this way himself, and to lead others to such obedience. To see in the passage an allusion to his coming death as an act by which eschatological judgment and salvation would be effected, and this the realization of the total intention of the Scriptures, is surely unjustified. No such intent of Matthew is evidenced by the context of the verse. It seems likely, therefore, that the scholars holding to positions

1) and 2), as summarized above, are nearer a true understanding of the verse than those adhering to 3) and 4).

We conclude, then, that Jesus' attitude toward the written law, as presented by Matthew, is one of respect and obedience toward its true requirements. He fulfilled it as it was meant by God to be fulfilled.

Jesus as the Second Moses

From many indications it is clear that Matthew saw Jesus as the second Moses, who was expected at the time of the end.

We learn from the disciples' reply to Jesus' question at Caesarea Philippi, "Who do men say that I am?" (Mark 8:27; cf. Matt. 16:13), that the Jews of that day were accustomed to think of certain great worthies of the past as returning at or near the end of the age to assist the nation in realizing its hopes and its place in the plan of God. It would not have been altogether strange if, besides "John the Baptist," "Elijah," "Jeremiah," or "one of the prophets," "Moses" had been mentioned.

The passing of the centuries had established not only the law at the heart of Judaism but its giver as well. Philo, the Jewish philosopher of Alexandria, in his *Life of Moses* portrays Moses as the perfect king, history's greatest law-giver, high priest, and prophet. He speaks of him is such extravagant language that he virtually deifies him. In the *Assumption of Moses* Joshua tells Moses that no ordinary grave is sufficient to receive him: "thy sepulchre is from the rising to the setting sun, and from the south to the confines of the north: all the world is thy sepulchre" (11:8). He is called in this work "God's chief prophet throughout the earth, the most perfect teacher in the world" (11:16). Josephus extolled Moses as the best of all lawgivers, whose leader and counselor was God (*Against Apion* 2:154-75). In another passage he says, "our lawgiver was a divine man" (*Antiq.* 3:180). Passages in the Midrashim claim that Moses was half man and half God. The tendency toward glorification was so strong that some rabbis felt it necessary to attempt to counter it lest monotheism be threatened.[14]

With the exaltation of Moses and the idealizing of his times as the greatest period of Hebrew history arose the belief that such times would return. Moses would reappear to play a part in the liberation of God's people and the inauguration of the messianic kingdom. This belief was made possible by another: that Moses, like Enoch and Elijah, had been taken up into heaven without tasting of death.[15]

Opinions varied concerning the exact role Moses would play in the future. By some it was thought that he would come as an eschatological prophet, to prepare the way for the Messiah's inauguration of the kingdom of God. This may be suggested in the Gospels in the story of the Transfiguration. Here Moses appears with Elijah, another way-preparer. Together with Jesus, the Messiah, they constitute the *dramatis personae* of the end time. A rabbinic tradition of uncertain date also associates Moses and Elijah in a return in the messianic period. Here God says to Moses, "In the time to come, when I bring Elijah, the prophet, unto them, the two of you shall come together." The Jerusalem Targum on Exodus 12:42 says: "Moses will go out from the midst of the desert, and the King Messiah from the midst of Rome. The one will walk on the summit of a

[14] On the place of Moses in Jewish thought of the New Testament period see Howard M. Teeple, *The Mosaic Eschatological Prophet* (Philadelphia: Society of Biblical Literature, 1957); J. Jeremias in G. Kittel (ed.), *Theologisches Wörterbuch zum Neuen Testament* (Stuttgart, 1933 —), IV, 852-78; R. Schnackenburg, "Die Erwartung des 'Propheten' nach dem Neuen Testament und den Qumran-Texten," in Kurt Aland *et al.* (eds.), *Studia Evangelica* (Berlin, 1959), pp. 622-39; H. J. Schoeps, *Theologie und Geschichte des Judenchristentums* (Tübingen, 1949), pp. 87 ff.; N. Wieder, "The 'Law-interpreter' of the Sect of the Dead Sea Scrolls: The Second Moses," *Journal of Jewish Studies,* IV (1953), 158-75.

[15] See Teeple, *op. cit.,* pp. 41 ff.

cloud, the other also will walk on the summit of a cloud, and the Word of Yahweh will walk between the two, and they will go together." Moses is made to appear in the desert, apparently to lead into the messianic kingdom the generation which died in the wilderness at the time of the Exodus. Though this source dates to the fifth century A.D., it probably reflects beliefs of earlier times as well.[16]

Whether some Jews at the time of the author of Matthew believed that Moses would return as the Messiah is uncertain. It is possible that Rev. 11: 3-13, which seems to rest on a Jewish source, reflects this view.[17] To judge from the type of miracles (power to hinder rainfall, to turn waters into blood, and to bring plagues upon the earth) the prophesying witnesses are intended to represent Elijah and Moses. But they seem to be more than forerunners. They are said to be olive trees and lampstands (cf. Zech. 4) and to have power to consume their enemies by fire from their mouths (cf. IV Ezra 13: 10 ff.). These are messianic symbols. The fact that there are two figures (Messiahs?) here is no obstacle, for the doctrine of two Messiahs is clearly expressed in the Dead Sea Scrolls.[18] But the interpretation of these figures as Messiahs is put in some doubt by the fact that nowhere in contemporary or near-contemporary Jewish literature as such is the returning Moses repre-

[16] Solomon Zeitlin believes that the idea of a second coming of Moses was not known to Jews of the pre-Christian period or the first centuries of the Christian era, though it was common belief in the late Middle Ages. For the opposing view and an exchange of opinion on the subject see N. Wieder, "The Idea of a Second Coming of Moses," *Jewish Quarterly Review,* XLVI (1955-56), 356-66. Against Zeitlin's conclusion see also Schoeps, *op. cit.,* p. 96.

[17] So Teeple, *op. cit.,* pp. 44 ff. and William H. Brownlee in Krister Stendahl (ed.), *The Scrolls and the New Testament* (New York: Harper & Bros., 1957), p. 49.

[18] Karl Georg Kuhn, "The Two Messiahs of Aaron and Israel," in Stendahl (ed.), *ibid.,* pp. 54-65.

sented as a (or the) Messiah.[19] Such a belief did, however, exist among the Samaritans.[20]

More common than the belief that Moses would actually return was the expectation that God would raise up a prophet *like* Moses at or near the end of the age. It was chiefly Deut. 18:15, 18 which formed the basis of this hope. Though some Jews held that the promise of Deut. 18 had been fulfilled in the appearance of some historical person (like Joshua, Jeremiah, Ezra), others looked for this figure in connection with the coming of the messianic age. One example may be cited here. The sectarians of Qumran expected the coming of a prophet and two Messiahs (one priestly and the other lay).[21] That this prophet was regarded as the one predicted in Deut. 18 seems probable from the fact that Deut. 18:18 is quoted in a collection of messianic *testimonia* found at Qumran.[22] It is possible that the men of Qumran held that their departed Teacher of Righteousness would return as this prophet like Moses.[23] What role this coming prophet was to play is not clear in the Qumran texts. But that he was regarded as a way-preparer for the Messiahs seems obvious.

The belief that the Messiah (or one of the Messiahs), while not Moses come again, would be *like* Moses, was likewise held by many. In view of the dominance of the figure of Moses in Judaism as the great deliverer and lawgiver, it was inevitable that the last deliverer should be characterized in terms of the first. The exodus from Egypt and associated events were viewed as the prototype of the messianic salvation. The men of Qumran withdrew into the wilderness, entered into a "new

[19] Joachim Jeremias, *op. cit.*, IV, 861.
[20] Teeple, *op. cit.*, p. 63 f.
[21] Millar Burrows, *More Light on the Dead Sea Scrolls* (New York: Viking Press, 1958), p. 315.
[22] *Ibid.*, p. 400.
[23] *Ibid.*, p. 334. Cf. R. Schnackenburg, *op. cit.*, pp. 633 ff.

covenant" there, arranged their settlement after the pattern of the Mosaic camp of the desert, and sought to prepare themselves for the second deliverance by obedience to the law as interpreted by their great Teacher. They devoted themselves, according to the ancient pattern of the wars of Yahweh, to preparations for fighting the great and final battles of the Lord. They seem to have expected at first that their sojourn in the wilderness would last forty years.

In the rabbinic literature we find often, "as the first deliverer [Moses], so the last deliverer [the Messiah]." The parallels between Moses and the Messiah were developed in detail.[24] As the first deliverer rode on an ass (Ex. 4:20), so will the last (Zech. 9:9). As the first brought down manna from heaven (Ex. 16:4), so will the last (Midrash on Ps. 72:16). As the first made a spring of water to arise (Num. 20:11), so will the last (Joel 3:18). As Moses was educated at the court of the Pharaoh, so will the Messiah before his appearance dwell in the capital of his enemies (Rome). As beside Moses stood Aaron, so beside the Messiah will stand Elijah. There is evidence that this type of comparison was being drawn in rabbinic circles as early as the time of Rabbi Akiba (*ca.* 90-135), though it was considerably more common in later centuries. Josephus' references to messianic pretenders who summoned their followers into the wilderness in order to lead them into the promised land show that attempts at conscious duplication of the Mosaic situation were made in the first century.

The second great deliverer, like the first, was to be a teacher and lawgiver. This aspect of his work, adumbrated in the Old Testament, is developed in the intertestamental and the rab-

[24] See Paul Volz, *Die Eschatologie der jüdischen Gemeinde im neutestamentlichen Zeitalter* (Tübingen, 1934), p. 370; Joachim Jeremias, *op. cit.*, IV, 864 f.

binic literature.[25] Especially stressed is his great wisdom. In I Enoch it is said that he is "mighty in all the secrets of righteousness" (49:2) and that "his mouth shall pour forth all the secrets of wisdom and counsel" (51:3). In the Psalms of Solomon he is called "a righteous king, taught of God," who will "bless the people of the Lord with wisdom and gladness," and whose words are "more refined than costly gold" (17:23 ff.). It is not indicated what the content of his instruction will be. But in view of the close connection between wisdom and the Torah in Judaism (cf. Sirach 24:3-23), one may safely conclude that he was regarded as expounding, in part at least, the secrets of the Torah.

It is thus in the rabbinic literature. Typical is the Targum on Ps. 45:10 f.: "The peoples of the kingdoms will come to greet thy [the Messiah's] face and to honor thee, while the book of the Torah, which is written with gold from Ophir, lies at thy right hand. Hear, O congregation of Israel, the Torah of his mouth, and look upon the wonders of his doing, and incline thine ear to the words of the Torah." In a Midrash on Ps. 2, Rabbi Judah (*ca.* 350) is quoted as having said, "All these consolations which are comprised in the decree of the king of all kings [i.e., in Ps. 2:7] shall be realized in the king, the Messiah; and why will all this happen? Because he will occupy himself with the Torah." [26] It was frequently said that in the messianic

[25] See W. D. Davies, *Torah in the Messianic Age and/or the Age to Come* (Philadelphia: Society of Biblical Literature, 1952), pp. 29 ff.

[26] The two examples are quoted from Hermann L. Strack and Paul Billerbeck, *Kommentar zum Neuen Testament aus Talmud und Midrash* (München, 1922-56), IV, 1, and III, 19. It should be borne in mind that "Torah" meant to the Jew "teaching" or "instruction." It was used both for the books of Moses and the teaching contained in them and other parts of the Scriptures. "Torah" is not properly translated by the word "law" (see Solomon Schechter, *Some Aspects of Rabbinic Theology* [New York: The Macmillan Co., 1909], pp. 117 ff.). This will be important when we come to consider the concept of Jesus as the giver of a new Torah.

age the inexplicable demands of the Torah would be made plain.

Though the Torah in Judaism was in general held to be immutable, there is clear evidence that some alterations of it were expected in the messianic age. Enactments concerning certain festivals and some regulations governing clean and unclean things would be changed.[27] Some bits of evidence lead beyond the suggestion that the Messiah would modify the Torah to the position that he would abrogate it and introduce a new Torah. The Covenanters of Qumran, for example, held that their laws and practices had validity only until the coming of the prophet and the two Messiahs,[28] after which it appears that the priestly Messiah would proclaim a new and final law. A rabbinic passage asserts: "The Torah which a man learned in this world is vanity compared with the Torah of the Messiah." Another says, "The Holy One, blessed be He, will sit in Paradise and give instruction, and all the righteous will sit before him and all the hosts of heaven will stand on His right and the sun and stars on His left; and the Holy One, blessed be He, interprets to them the grounds of a new Torah which the Holy One, blessed be He, will give to them by the hand of King Messiah." [29]

To what extent the Torah of the Messiah was thought of as really new is a moot point. Strack and Billerbeck thought that the rabbis meant to say only that the Messiah would expound the old Torah in a new and complete way, so firm was the doctrine of the immutability of the Torah in Judaism.[30] W. D. Davies thinks this judgment "errs on the side of caution," that even in the few passages from rabbinic sources we have the statement that the Messiah's Torah is new should be taken seriously. He rightly sees a duality of emphasis here, which,

[27] See W. D. Davies, *op. cit.,* pp. 54 ff.
[28] 1QS IX.10 f.; CD XIV.18 f.
[29] These passages are cited by Davies, *op. cit.,* pp. 71, 74.
[30] *Op. cit.,* IV, 1.

we might say, is not so much contradictory as paradoxical. Such an emphasis made it possible for the New Testament to present Christianity "as a movement which not only denies the old Torah on one level, and affirms and fulfils it on another, but also introduces a New Torah." [31]

The stage is now set for a consideration of the Gospel of Matthew. To what extent, if any, did the writer of this Gospel see Jesus against the background of Jewish speculation concerning Moses?

Our examination of the Christology of the Gospel of Matthew in Chapter II indicated clearly that the writer saw Jesus as the kind of Messiah characterized by the terms "Son of Man," "Son of God," and "God with us" for the salvation of men. He belongs to the realm of deity, though he lived on earth as a human being. He was supernaturally born. He has been exalted by the Father to universal authority. He is the final Judge of men and Ruler of the coming kingdom. We noted in Chapter III that the multitudes who did not understand who he really was regarded him as a prophet, but the disciples, to whom God had revealed his real identity, knew that he was the unique Son of the Father. In view of this Christology, it is obvious that the writer of the Gospel of Matthew did not regard Jesus as the eschatological prophet like Moses, expected by some, or as Moses himself come again. In the transfiguration scene (17:1-8) Moses is represented as appearing with Jesus, the Messiah-Son of God; Moses is not the Messiah. Our writer probably would agree with the author of the book of Hebrews: "Moses was faithful in all God's house as a servant . . . but Christ was faithful over God's house as a son" (3:5, 6).

It is possible, however, that Matthew wishes to represent Jesus, the second Deliverer, as in many respects *like* the first.

[31] *Op. cit.*, p. 91.

Typological thinking, so common (as we have seen) in Judaism, is to be found also in the New Testament.[32]

B. W. Bacon believed that the second Moses concept was stamped on the pattern of organization of the Gospel of Matthew, that the author divided his work into five major parts or "books," in conscious imitation of the Pentateuch.[33] Bacon found in each "book" a narrative introduction and a discourse, the kind of alternation of material one finds in the Pentateuch. A transitional formula, found five times (7:28; 11:1; 13:53; 19:1; 26:1), marks off the "books" and joins them to each other. The five-book structure, said he, is introduced by a Preamble (Chs. 1 and 2) and concluded with an Epilogue (Chs. 26-28). He regarded the author as a converted rabbi and Christian legalist, who wished to furnish the church with an orderly compendium of the commandments of Jesus, a "new law," modeled after the Pentateuch, which would help stem the tide of antinomianism then threatening to destroy the church. The teaching of Jesus is a new *Halakah* (code of conduct) with a higher origin and sanction than that advocated by the Pharisees. It is not, however, discontinuous with the old law. Jesus, as the second Moses, shows what the old law really requires.

[32] Robert M. Grant asserts that "the New Testament method of interpreting the Old was generally that of typology" (*The Bible in the Church* [New York: The Macmillan Co., 1948], p. 42). See Chapter IV of this work. The attempt of P. Nepper-Christensen, *Das Matthäusevangelium* (Aarhus, 1958), Ch. VI, to deny all typological representation to Matthew is scarcely convincing. Its coverage of the data is too limited and the material is not seen in the perspective of the Jewish background.

[33] See *Studies in Matthew* (New York: Henry Holt & Co., 1930), pp. 265 ff. He identifies the "books" as follows: Book I, Concerning Discipleship (Chs. 3-7); Book II, Concerning Apostleship (Chs. 8-10); Book III, Concerning the Hiding of the Revelation (Chs. 11-13); Book IV, Concerning Church Administration (Chs. 14-18); Book V, Concerning the Judgment (Chs. 19-25).

Bacon's outline of the Gospel has been widely influential.[34] However, a number of scholars have opposed the division into five "books" as a fanciful construction imposed on the contents of the Gospel.[35] It is said that there are six, rather than five discourses,[36] and that Bacon's outline reduces Matthew's Passion story to an epilogue, when in reality it is the climax of his book. One scholar suggests that the Gospel is really a new Hexateuch, rather than a Pentateuch.[37]

It remains doubtful whether Matthew meant the organization of his material to suggest the five books of Moses. But there can be little doubt that the career and work of Moses shimmers under the text of the Gospel and suggests again and again that Jesus is like, though greater than, Moses.

Details of the Matthean birth and infancy stories clearly reflect influence of traditions concerning Moses. Josephus (*Antiq.* 2:205) reports that one of the sacred scribes of Egypt predicted to the king the birth of "one who would abase the sovereignty of the Egyptians . . . and win everlasting renown." Correspondingly, the wise men from the East and the Jewish scribes anticipated the birth of Jesus, the latter pinpointing Bethlehem as the place of his nativity (Matt. 2:1-6). In both cases the kings are said to have reacted to the information by ordering the slaughter of male children. Furthermore, the fathers of both deliverers are instructed and reassured in

[34] It has been accepted essentially by F. W. Green, *The Gospel According to St. Matthew* (Oxford: The Clarendon Press, 1936); G. D. Kilpatrick, *The Origins of the Gospel According to St. Matthew* (Oxford: The Clarendon Press, 1946); Krister Stendahl, *The School of St. Matthew* (Uppsala, 1954); Sherman E. Johnson, "The Gospel According to St. Matthew," *The Interpreter's Bible,* VII.

[35] Günther Bornkamm and Gerhard Barth, *op. cit.,* pp. 32 (note 2), 143. Austin Farrer, *St. Matthew and St. Mark* (Westminster: Dacre Press, 1954), pp. 179 ff.; Edgar J. Goodspeed, *Matthew—Apostle and Evangelist* (Philadelphia: John C. Winston Co., 1959), pp. 26 ff.

[36] By Goodspeed, for example.

[37] Austin Farrer, *op. cit.,* Ch. XI.

dreams (*Antiq.* 2:212 ff.; Matt. 2:13, 19, 22). Joseph at length is told in language obviously borrowed from Exod. 4:19 that the persecutors are dead and that it is safe to return home (Matt. 2:20). The coming of Jesus out of Egypt is explicitly paralleled with the Exodus under Moses and seen as a fulfillment of prophecy (Matt. 2:15).

In the story of the temptation of Jesus Matthew carries farther the typologizing tendency already at work in the materials used by him. Mark and Luke speak only of forty days but Matthew of "forty days and forty nights" of fasting (cf. Exod. 34:28; Deut. 9:9, 11, 18).

Matthew's "mountain" (5:1; 8:1—Luke in 6:17 has "a level place"), on which the new Torah of Jesus (Matt. 5-7) was delivered, seems to be the counterpart of the mountain of God from which the old Torah came (Exod. 19 ff.). The mention elsewhere in the Gospel of Matthew of "mountains" as places of revelation (17:1; 24:3; 28:16) strengthens the impression that mount Sinai and the Moses stories have deeply affected the tradition about Jesus.[38]

The content of much of the Sermon on the Mount has in view the relationship of Jesus to Moses and the latter's interpreters. Here it is shown, as we have seen above, that Jesus does not contradict or abrogate Moses but shows what his Torah, when rightly understood, really requires of men. The second Moses, by so much as he is greater than the first, can declare the will and the purposes of God with absolute authority: "Listen to him." (Matt. 17:5; cf. 28:18-20.)

Not only Jesus' words but also his deeds accredit him as the second Moses. Ten deeds of power are brought together in

[38] Nepper-Christensen, *op. cit.,* pp. 173 ff., denies any theological significance to the mention of mountains in the Gospel of Matthew. He comments on the mountainous topography of the country and concludes that "mountain" here is more a geographical than a theological datum. This is of a piece with his general denial of typological thought in Matthew.

Chs. 8-9 from various contexts in Mark. One thinks of the passage in the Mishnah (Pirke Aboth 5:4) where it is said, "Ten wonders were wrought for our fathers in Egypt and ten at the Sea." It was expected, as we noted above, that the Messiah would be like Moses in the working of miracles.

It is possible, but undemonstrable, that our author thinks of Moses as the type of Jesus in suffering. Jeremias believes that in the rabbinic literature and in the Jewish source lying behind Rev. 11:3 ff. there are indications that Moses was regarded as a suffering, atoning figure.[39] This seems suggested in Deuteronomy (3:23 ff.; 9:8 f., 25 ff.).[40] However this may be, it is clear that the Servant of the Lord concept of the book of Isaiah has deeply affected Matthew's thought about Jesus.[41] The Jesus of this Gospel is the Savior of men from sin; or, to put it positively, he makes the higher righteousness possible for them. His "blood of the covenant" is poured out "for the forgiveness of sins" (26:28). It is only in discipleship to the gentle-and-lowly-in-heart (Matt. 11:29), suffering-and-dying Jesus that the true righteousness, i.e., inner goodness, is to be found and the kingdom of heaven entered. The Passion and Resurrection stories cannot be thrown into an "Epilogue," as B. W. Bacon does. The Jesus of Matthew's Gospel is not only a teacher but definitely a Savior, as indeed was Moses!

Is the author of the Gospel of Matthew "a Christian legalist"? Is salvation for him to be gained by obeying the new Torah of Jesus? Is this Torah regarded as a new *Halakah?*

An affirmative answer is impossible in the light of the total sweep of Matthew's thought. His doctrine of salvation revolves around four centers, not just one: knowing, believing, being, and doing.

[39] *Op. cit.,* IV, 867.

[40] See Albrecht Oepke in *Theologisches Wörterbuch zum Neuen Testament,* IV, 616.

[41] See pp. 78 ff.

We noted in Chapter III that Matthew holds that the Father has revealed his truth to the Son and that the Son in turn reveals it to the disciples (11:27-30). It is also said that the Father in heaven has revealed to Peter the true identity of Jesus (16:17). Every disciple must *know* the mysteries of the kingdom of heaven. Among these are: God's purpose for mankind, who Jesus is, what he is doing in the world, what he will do at the last, and what the basis of admission to the kingdom of heaven is. The enemies of Jesus and the multitudes outside understood none of these "mysteries." But the disciples had seeing eyes and hearing ears. At times they had only "little faith" in Jesus, but at others they fell down at his feet in worship and confession of his true deity (14:33). Knowing and believing go hand in hand in this Gospel.

Inseparably related to these are being and doing. The disciple must be inwardly good, not externally correct. God wants freedom from anger, lust, and hypocrisy, and abounding generosity of spirit toward persecutors and enemies. He desires "mercy and not sacrifice." Nothing short of complete love for God and one's fellow men will suffice. "You, therefore, must be perfect, as your heavenly Father is perfect" (5:48). Perfection here, in the light of the context, clearly means inward goodness, sincerity, integrity, and benevolence, not absolute sinlessness.[42]

But inner goodness is not enough. It must lead to loving acts of service. This is most graphically set forth in the parable concerning the Judgment (25:31-46). It is not the pious but the actively benevolent who are here admitted to the kingdom of the Son of Man. The food, the drink, the clothes, the loving concern for the sick and the imprisoned—by these is a man really known. The heart of love and the hands of service are the unmistakable marks of the Christian disciple. Jesus, the

[42] So Frederick C. Grant, in an incisive discussion of the term in *The Earliest Gospel* (Nashville: Abingdon Press, 1943), pp. 218 ff.

Son of Man, has so made himself one with the suffering and needy of the world that in ministering to them one really ministers to him who has shared their lot.[43] The higher righteousness and perfection, about which Matthew talks, mean simply being and acting like Jesus.

Matthew was no legalist who wanted to turn Jesus' teaching into a code of conduct to replace the law of Moses and Pharisaic tradition. He wanted to raise up disciples of Jesus—men who would have his spirit and do his works in the world.

[43] For a splendid interpretation of this parable see Théo Preiss, *Life in Christ* (Naperville, Ill.: Alec R. Allenson, Inc., 1954), Ch. III.

[5]

Matthew's Jesus and First-Century Christianity

MARTIN DIBELIUS begins his book on Jesus with the assertion that Christian faith rests on the conviction that in Jesus' words, deeds, death, and resurrection God has revealed himself to men. History, he says, looks at Jesus from an entirely different point of view. It attempts to relate Jesus to his background, to describe the nature and course of his ministry, to affix the causes of his death, and to view his achievements in the light of contemporary religious philosophies and movements.[1]

It is evident that Matthew—and indeed all the evangelists—writes about Jesus from the perspective of faith. Matthew clearly believes that in Jesus' words God is speaking, in his deeds God is acting, and in his death and resurrection God is rescuing man from his sins. He presents Jesus as "God with us" and active for the redemption of mankind. The Gospel of Matthew is not a book of history but a "gospel," the "good news" concerning what God has done and will do in Jesus Christ "for us men and our salvation." It is written from faith to faith.

It has been our aim in this book to identify the distinctive

[1] *Jesus* (Philadelphia: Westminster Press, 1949), pp. 1 ff.

emphases in Matthew's portrait of Jesus. But heretofore we have looked only at separate aspects. It is now time to step farther from the canvas, contemplate the whole, and relate it, so far as time will permit, to other characterizations of Jesus. Finally, we shall ask what such a picture of Jesus would have meant to the church for which Matthew created it.

Our clew to Matthew's perspective was found in 28:18 ff.: "All authority in heaven and on earth has been given to me. . . ." Parallel to this passage are the words of 11:27: "All things have been delivered to me by my Father. . . ." Jesus' inherent right and manifest capability to fulfill the role he undertook were derived from God.

It may be helpful to attempt to catch up in a brief statement the chief characteristics of Matthew's representation of Jesus. Such epitomes are dangerous in that they inevitably leave out much that should be included, but they are necessary in that they assist the mind in encompassing large amounts of data. Perspective is indispensable to understanding.

Such a statement might be:

Jesus is the divine-human, God-sent, eschatological Deliverer (the Messiah, Son of God, Son of Man, suffering Servant, second Moses), by whose life, death, and resurrection mankind is delivered from the bondage of sin. He is the giver of a new Torah (inherent in, explicative of, and the consummation of the old Torah) and the God-appointed inaugurator of the coming kingdom of heaven. Knowledge concerning him (who he is, what he has said and done, what he will do), faith in him, and loyalty to him (by radical obedience to his Torah and imitation of his acts of loving service) will result in admission by him to the heavenly kingdom soon to be established.

A few comments on this summary may be in order.

First, it draws together the major titles by which Jesus is known in the Gospel of Matthew. They combine to reveal Jesus as the supernatural endtime Deliverer, who, though truly in the flesh, could be known for what he really was only by revelation from the Father. This Jesus was unique from the time of his birth. He was publicly declared by the Father at the baptism to be his beloved (only) Son and his true identity was revealed to the disciples during the course of his ministry. After his resurrection he appeared on a mountain in Galilee as future King and Judge of all men (the Son of Man) in a position alongside the Father and the Holy Spirit. His authority is represented as rooting in his identity—in his basic and unique relationship to God. He is shown to have possessed this authority during his lifetime (11:27), not simply after his resurrection (28:18).

If this characterization of Matthew's Christology is accurate, it is impossible to agree with B. W. Bacon that the Synoptic Gospels all present an "exaltation" or a sort of "apotheosis" Christology—that Jesus is regarded in the Synoptics as "a man whose earthly ministry is the basis and ground of his exaltation to Lordship in heaven." [2] Not even in Mark, the earliest of the Gospels, is such a Christology to be found.[3]

Furthermore, Oscar Cullmann is scarcely right in his contention that the Synoptics present a Messiah-Son of God, and not a Son of Man, Christology.[4] At least this is not true for Matthew. We have seen how dominant in his thinking about Jesus the role suggested in the Son of Man concept is: Jesus is the kind of Messiah suggested (in part) by the term "Son of Man."

Second, this summary recognizes the influence of the second Moses thought on the Gospel of Matthew but avoids excessive

[2] *The Gospel of the Hellenists* (New York: Henry Holt & Co., 1933), pp. 101 ff.

[3] See Vincent Taylor, *The Gospel According to St. Mark* (New York: St. Martin's Press, 1952), pp. 120 ff.

[4] *Die Christologie des Neuen Testaments* (Tübingen, 1957), pp. 167 ff.

emphasis (as in Bacon and others) on one phase of Moses' work: that of teacher and lawgiver. Matthew sees Jesus' death and resurrection as a means of overcoming sin. His Jesus is not simply the giver of a new Torah. The Passion story is a climactically important part of his Gospel. It is not an addendum to five books of "law."

Third, Jesus' teachings are here represented, not as contradictory to the law and the prophets, but as explicative of and complementary to them. Jesus wishes to show what the law and the prophets really require (inner goodness, love, and mercy). He affirms the validity of the Old Testament in its true meaning. We cannot agree with Bornkamm and his students that Matthew's Jesus is represented as moving in the orbit of Pharisaic scribalism and accepting basically the validity of Pharisaic tradition, on the one hand, while criticizing the Pharisees' hypocrisy, misuse of tradition, and failure to grasp the heart of the law and the prophets, on the other. Matthew feels that the Pharisees have missed *altogether* the true meaning of the Scriptures.

Fourth, this summary recognizes the strongly eschatological character of the theology of Matthew. The near coming of the Son of Man for the judgment of the world stands in the foreground of his thinking, as his expansion of Mark's little apocalypse (Mark 13; Matt. 24-25) clearly shows. We agree with J. A. T. Robinson [5] that Matthew (and his special tradition) considerably accentuates the eschatological element in the teaching of Jesus.

Fifth, Matthew's strong emphasis on the importance of knowledge in salvation is recognized and given its proper emphasis in the structure of Matthew's thought. The disciples are not put in a favorable light because of the reverence in which they were held in the author's time. Matthew regards

[5] *Jesus and His Coming* (Nashville: Abingdon Press, 1957), *passim.*

the disciples as members of an elect community to which divine mysteries have been communicated—the truth necessary for salvation.

Sixth, the emphasis in the Gospel of Matthew on *doing* is related in our summary to *knowing, believing,* and *being.* The Jesus of this Gospel is not the giver of a new *Halakah* (code of conduct), obedience to which will result in eschatological salvation. It is insisted that one must become good within and that out of such inner goodness will flow good deeds. The true disciple is like Jesus both inwardly and outwardly.

There remains the task of setting Matthew's Christology in the context of the thought of the early church as a whole and indicating the revelance of this Christology for the times out of which it came. However, such an achievement seems quite beyond the ability of contemporary New Testament scholars. Some tentative suggestions are offered here, but the writer is well aware of their vulnerability. It perhaps should be repeated that the primary objective of these studies has been to define as sharply as possible the character of Matthew's portrait of Jesus. The explanation of the reasons for such a portrait may or may not have validity. Here only hypotheses seem possible at the moment.

The characteristics of Matthew's Christology which should prove most useful in affixing its position are the following: (1) the use of the second Moses speculation; (2) the explanation of Christianity as true Judaism, in fact, the consummation of Judaism; (3) the emphasis on understanding as essential to salvation; (4) the prominence of the Son of Man ideology and its fusion with the Son of God concept especially.

A type of thought which comes close to the theology of the Gospel of Matthew is to be found in the address of Stephen before his martyrdom (Acts 7) and in the Qumran texts (the Dead Sea Scrolls).

Stephen's address and the theology behind it have been studied recently by Marcel Simon[6] and somewhat earlier by William Manson.[7] Oscar Cullmann[8] has been calling attention of late to the importance of the theological point of view represented by Stephen and the Hellenists, especially in relation to the theology of the Fourth Gospel and the book of Hebrews. It apparently has not yet been suggested that an affinity exists between the theology of Matthew and that of Stephen and the Hellenists. For the most part, only scattered connections between Matthew and the Qumran texts have been noted.[9] It is proposed to show here that considerable similarity in the overall theology of Matthew and these two groups does exist, however the affinities be explained.

It is becoming increasingly apparent that the Hellenists of Acts 6:1 ff. represent a kind of reforming or nonconformist Judaism, which was hotly opposed by the dominant Pharisaic and Sadducean religious leadership of the period. The term may mean "paganizing" (Simon) or "living after the manner of the Greeks" (Cullmann). It was probably an opprobrious

[6] *St. Stephen and the Hellenists in the Primitive Church* (London: Longmans, Green & Co., 1958). See also A. F. J. Klijn, "Stephen's Speech—Acts VII.2-53," *New Testament Studies,* IV (1957/58), 25-31.

[7] *The Epistle to the Hebrews* (London: Hodder and Stoughton Ltd., 1951), Ch. II.

[8] "A New Approach to the Interpretation of the Fourth Gospel," *Expository Times,* LXXI (1959), 8-12, 39-43. See also C. Spicq, "L'Épitre aux Hébreux, Apollos, Jean-Baptiste, les Hellénistes et Qumran," *Revue de Qumran,* I (1959), 365-90.

[9] E.g., in W. D. Davies, " 'Knowledge' in the Dead Sea Scrolls and Matthew 11:25-30," *Harvard Theological Review,* XLVI (1953), 113-39; Krister Stendahl, *The School of St. Matthew* (Uppsala, 1954); Bertil Gärtner, "The Habakkuk Commentary (DSH) and the Gospel of Matthew," *Studia Theologica,* VIII (1954), 1-24; Kurt Schubert, "The Sermon on the Mount and the Qumran Texts," in Krister Stendahl (ed.), *The Scrolls and the New Testament* (Harper and Brothers, 1957), Ch. VIII; C. Umhau Wolf, "The Gospel to the Essenes," *Biblical Research,* III (1958), 28-43.

epithet, first used by opponents. Whether these "off-beat" Jews had come from the Diaspora, as Simon thinks, or were indigenous to Palestine, as Cullmann holds, cannot be certainly determined. They clearly lived as a distinct community at the time of the rise of the church in Jerusalem. Many of them, as we see from the book of Acts, were converted to Christianity and apparently brought into the church their radical views. It is significant that when the heavy hand of persecution fell on the young church, the fury was directed at the Hellenists and not at the apostles, who apparently were in the main conformists (Acts 3:1; 8:1).

It is unnecessary to say much here about the Qumran community.[10] It obviously represents sectarian Judaism. These sectarians withdrew to the Wilderness of Judaea in the second century before Christ and followed an interpretation of the Old Testament and a discipline quite at variance from the dominant Pharisaic and Sadducean patterns. Their outlook was strongly eschatological. They regarded themselves as the righteous remnant, the people in true covenant relationship with God, to whom he would give the messianic kingdom. They were militaristic in spirit, holding that God would use them to defeat the enemies of Israel in a great forty-year eschatological war. For this reason some have held them to be the Zealots who waged the great rebellion against Rome in A.D. 66-73.[11] Their doctrines and books were jealously guarded

[10] For authoritative treatments of the discoveries and their interpretation see: Millar Burrows, *The Dead Sea Scrolls* (New York: The Viking Press, 1955) and *More Light on the Dead Sea Scrolls* (New York: The Viking Press, 1958); Frank Moore Cross, *The Ancient Library of Qumran and Modern Biblical Studies* (Garden City, New York: Doubleday, 1958); J. T. Milik, *Ten Years of Discovery in the Wilderness of Judaea* (Naperville, Illinois: Alec R. Allenson, Inc., 1959).

[11] Cecil Roth, *The Historical Background of the Dead Sea Scrolls* (Oxford: Basil Blackwell, 1958).

from outsiders. To become a member one had to make a radical renunciation of the world and undergo initiation in stages. Their loyalty was centered in the law of Moses as interpreted by their great Teacher of Righteousness (or Right-Teacher).

Stephen's address is an indictment of official Judaism in the form of a tendentious summary of Israelite history. It points out that the Jews, through most of their past, have misunderstood and disobeyed the will of God. They have professed to honor Moses, but in reality they have opposed him from the beginning. Though God had sent him to be a "ruler and deliverer" (Acts 7:35), they repudiated him repeatedly, saying, "Who made you a ruler and judge over us?" (7:27, 35. Cf. vs. 39). They refused to obey the "living oracles" God gave Moses at Sinai and turned to ways of their own devising—to worship of the golden calf and to construction of a temple to replace the God-ordained tabernacle. Persisting farther in their willfulness, they persecuted and killed the prophets and now at last have betrayed and murdered the "Righteous One," the second Moses (7:37). They have not kept the divine law but have been "stiff-necked" and "uncircumcized in heart and ears," always resisting the Holy Spirit (7:51).

Judging from the charges laid against Stephen—that he spoke against the temple and the law and that he said that Jesus would destroy the temple and change the customs which Moses had established (6:13-14)—one can but conclude that Stephen viewed the future coming of Jesus as God's moment of judgment of the nation and its corrupt religious institutions and practices.

We turn now to specific comparisons between the theology of Matthew, on the one hand, and the views of Stephen and the Hellenists and the sectarians of Qumran, on the other. First, let us look at the use of the second Moses speculation.

We noted earlier how this type of thinking underlies the

birth and infancy stories of the Gospel of Matthew, the narrative of the temptation, the teaching from a "mountain," and the ten miracles of Chapters 8-9. The use of this motif is subtly introduced by Matthew; a touch here and there is sufficient to suggest the parallel between Jesus and Moses.

Stephen is more explicit. Deuteronomy 18:15, 18 is quoted (Acts 7:37) and the allusion to Jesus as the second Moses is patent. His point is that the will of God for the Jews has been made known through the two Moseses, but both revelations have been rejected. Stephen has been accused of despising Moses. He answers by devoting about half of his address to praise of this divinely appointed "ruler and deliverer" (7:35). He speaks of him in glowing terms: he was "beautiful before God" (7:20); he was "instructed in all the wisdom of the Egyptians, and he was mighty in his words and deeds" (7:22); he talked with an angel and "received living oracles to give to us" (7:38). He promised that God would send to Israel another like himself. It was not he but rather they who were anti-Mosaic. As their fathers had done to the first Moses, so had they done to the second, "the Righteous One," "the Son of Man," "the Lord Jesus."

It is clear from Peter's use of Deut. 18:15 (Acts 3:22) and the Moses-Jesus typology in the Fourth Gospel (6:25 ff.) that Stephen was not alone in the early church in employing the second Moses motif. But that it was an important concept for him, not a marginal one, is obvious from the strongly Mosaic character of the address. Simon rightly describes the speech as "Moseocentric."[12] Though the author of the Gospel of Matthew is more subtle, as we have said, the second Moses concept is important to him also.

We noted in Chapter IV that the concept of the second Moses appears in the Qumran texts. A prophet and two Messiahs

[12] *Op. cit.*, p. 45.

were expected. It seems clear from the quotation of Deut. 18:18 in the *Testimonia* that the prophet was expected precisely because of the prediction contained in this passage. Whether this coming prophet was thought to be the Teacher of Righteousness *redivivus* is an open question. What role the prophet was to play is not clear from the texts. About all that we can offer here is the simple assertion that the second Moses idea appears at Qumran.

Our second point of comparison lies in the explanation of Christianity as true (the true consummation of) Judaism. It follows from Stephen's characterization of Jesus as the second Moses that Christianity is regarded by him as the true Mosaic religion. Official Judaism has turned away from the Moses-Jesus line, from the "living oracles" of God (7:38), to practices and institutions of its own devising, notably, to worship in a temple rather than in the God-ordained, Moses-commissioned, and fathers-hallowed tabernacle (7:44-46). Though the Jews had received the law as delivered by angels, they had not kept it (7:53). Jesus, when he returns, will destroy the un-Mosaic temple and its sacrifices. He will thus free the law from its distortions and perversions. To Stephen there is no opposition or contradiction between the two Covenants, the Old and the New. Jesus is not against Moses; he rather affirms and shows the true meaning of Moses. His work is to clear away the distortions and preversions made by "stiff-necked" men.

Simon and Cullmann have shown that the rejection of temple worship lay at the heart of Stephen's attack on his persecutors and Cullmann has noted that criticism of the temple worship, as it was being carried on, was strongly voiced by the sectarians of Qumran. While Cullmann is aware that such criticism does not call into question the right of the temple as such to exist, he believes that the more radical attitude of Stephen is prepared for by Qumran.

Some elements in Stephen's address are obviously paralleled

in the Gospel of Matthew. There is in both a bitter attack on the religious leaders for distorting the Mosaic law and impeding the will of God by their perverse interpretations. Both Stephen and the author of the Gospel regard the religious officialdom as blind guides who lead others into the pit. God's judgment will fall upon them at the coming of the Son of Man.

But is not the ground of the criticism somewhat different? Matthew denounces the externalism of the Pharisees. Their righteousness consists in acts and ceremonies; it is not of the heart. They exalt the lesser matters of the law (practices and observances) and neglect "justice and mercy and faith." They teach as their doctrines the precepts of men (in the oral tradition). But is there any criticism of the temple, either in principle or in practice?

Though Matthew records the Q saying that "something greater than the temple is here" (12:6) and thrice includes references to destruction of the temple (24:2; 26:61; 27:40), there is no clear antipathy to the temple. In fact, the legitimacy of gifts at the altar is assumed and directions are given for making them truly effective (5:23-4).

The only material concerning the temple which offers a possible parallel to the general position represented by Stephen is contained in the story about payment of the temple tax (17:24-27). This story is peculiar to Matthew. Here the freedom of the sons of the kingdom (the disciples of Jesus) from obligation to support the temple by the payment of the tax is asserted by Jesus (17:26). But as a conciliatory gesture, so as "not to give offense to them" (17:27), Jesus makes provision for payment of the tax. On principle the disciple is free from the temple's claim; only practical considerations direct its support. This can hardly have been Jesus' attitude toward the temple, if the record of his cleansing of it and the attitudes there expressed (Mark 11:15-17) are to be trusted. Though he seems to have believed that the temple would pass away with the coming of the kingdom, he appears to have recognized its validity in the present order, that is, when cleansed of abuses impeding its true function.[13]

When one considers also that the story concerning payment of the tax represents Jesus as working a miracle of convenience, an act quite unrelated to his redemptive activity, and that it comes from a stratum of material in Matthew which is generally regarded as the least reliable historically of all Synoptic strata,[14] it is not hard to assign it to the early church. It is the sort of story that the Hellenists might have created or at least cherished. It denies the claim of the temple on principle but allows Christians to support it as a matter of concession. If the Hellenists had been more radical than this, it is hard to see how they could have lived in fellowship with the temple-attending apostles and their wing of the church. It is furthermore conceivable that Stephen overstated that Hellenist attitude toward the temple in the heat of the situation, or possibly that the record in Acts does not give their full position. However this may be, we seem to have in this story a point of contact with the Hellenist point of view. Had the temple still been standing when Matthew wrote, it is possible that more attempt to depreciate it would have been made. The real danger of the author's day was Pharisaic scribalism, and to this he devoted the brunt of his attack.

There can be no doubt that Stephen and Matthew are together in their view of the church as the true Israel. Both see the law of Moses as the living oracles of God, the man-made distortions of which Jesus had come to abolish. Stephen

[13] Ernest F. Scott, *The Crisis in the Life of Jesus* (New York: Charles Scribner's Sons, 1952), Chs. IV-V.

[14] Even by relatively conservative scholars like Archibald M. Hunter (*The Work and Words of Jesus* [Philadelphia: Westminster Press, 1950] p. 147) who calls the dozen or so narratives peculiar to the Gospel of Matthew "the least valuable bit of the Synoptic tradition."

would take no exception to Matthew's affirmation that Jesus came to fulfill the law by showing its true purpose and meaning, by carrying out in his own life its true demands (love and mercy), and by leading others through discipleship to him to a like fulfillment. The church is thus the Israel intended by God. The fate of official Israel is destruction.

A similar perspective dominates the Qumran texts. Here it is held that the Teacher of Righteousness has disclosed to his followers the true meaning of the law of Moses, an understanding quite different from that of official Judaism. It is believed, for example, that the temple and its offerings are being polluted by priests who have not observed the rules for ritual purity. Some of them have violated the laws concerning marriage in that they have been married more than once or are joined in wedlock with a niece. Here the men of Qumran have construed Gen. 1:27 and Lev. 18:13 very narrowly, in the latter passage even making the prohibition include nieces.[15] It is obvious that they regard their interpretation as alone true to the will of God as revealed to Moses.

The sect regarded itself as the true Israel. The Damascus Document clearly presents the sect as the Remnant, the righteous ones who had remained faithful to the Mosaic covenant, to whom God's promises would be fulfilled and through whom God's land would be cleansed from the stain of sin and guilt. In organization the community tried to model itself after the pattern of Israel during the wilderness period, as described in the book of Numbers.[16] The Manual of Discipline describes the annual renewal of the covenant (I. 7-II. 18). It consisted of prayers, thanksgiving, confession, and blessings and curses, the latter reminiscent of the ceremony at Ebal and Gerizim recorded in Deut. 27. Toward those outside—the "men of

[15] J. van der Ploeg, *The Excavations at Qumran* (London: Longmans, Green & Co., 1958), p. 125.
[16] Frank Moore Cross, *op. cit.*, pp. 55 ff.

Belial's lot," "the sons of darkness"—the most bitter attitudes were nurtured. Upon these God's eschatological judgment would be meted out. God would show his bounty in the gift of the messianic kingdom to this righteous Remnant.

It is evident that the perspective in the Qumran texts is not widely different from that in the speech of Stephen and in the Gospel of Matthew. In all three of the circles represented there is an "in" group and an "out" group, with ultimate victory promised to those inside. There are strong differences, of course, a major point being, as Stendahl has shown,[17] that the Christians held that their Messiah already had come and the end events thus had begun, while the men of Qumran waited for the eschatological events to commence. But there is a striking similarity in the over-all understanding of their position as the eschatological people of God.

The third point of comparison concerns the place of understanding in salvation. Stephen expressly states that failure to understand, as well as deliberate disobedience, lay at the bottom of Israel's rejection of Moses: "He supposed that his brethren understood that God was giving them deliverance by his hand, but they did not understand" (Acts 7:25). This doubly expressed affirmation of their lack of understanding is striking. Why they did not understand is not explained. One thinks of Peter's comment after Pentecost to the effect that his hearers and their rulers crucified Jesus "in ignorance" (Acts 3:17). But he also said that Jesus was "crucified and killed by the hands of lawless men" (2:23). The mind and the will are thus included in the explanation of the crucifixion by both early preachers.

Matthew's treatment of the place of understanding in salvation is not surprising in view of emphases within and without Judaism in the first century.

[17] *The Scrolls and the New Testament,* Ch. I.

That the Elect have been given special knowledge of the purposes of God is deeply imbedded in Judaism, and especially in apocalyptic Judaism. The non-apocalyptic Wisdom of Jesus the Son of Sirach (Ecclesiasticus) presents Israel as the place of abode of the divine Wisdom, Wisdom having first vainly sought a resting place among the Gentiles (Ch. 24). In the book of Daniel (the first great apocalypse) divine mysteries are communicated to various persons in dreams and visions, and the interpretation of these is made known to Daniel. The purpose of the entire book is to disclose to the Elect, who were suffering under the tyrant Antiochus Epiphanes, knowledge concerning the purposes of God with respect to eschatological deliverance. In the Psalms of Solomon the Messiah is characterized as "a righteous king, taught of God," who "will bless the people of the Lord with wisdom and gladness" (17:40). In I Enoch the Elect are said to be recipients of special wisdom imparted by the Son of Man (46:3; 48:1; 49:1 ff.).

In the Qumran texts much is said about the special knowledge possessed by the Teacher of Righteousness and his followers. The Teacher is said to have received his teaching from the mouth of God (1QpHab II.2). To him "God made known all the mysteries of the words of his servants the prophets" (1QpHab VII. 4-5). In the Thanksgiving Hymns the speaker (perhaps the Teacher of Righteousness) claims that God has revealed to him "wonderful mysteries" which he imparts to others (1QH I. 21; II. 13; IV. 27-29). It is clear that these "wonderful mysteries" concern the purposes of God for the time of the end. It is said in the Habakkuk Commentary that though God had commanded Habakkuk to write down the things that were to come upon the last generation, he did not make known unto him "the fulfillment of the epoch." This had been revealed to the Teacher of Righteousness (1QpHab VII. 1-5). The Teacher thus had knowledge withheld from Habakkuk himself.

There has been much discussion of the question whether it

is proper to speak of the theology of the Qumran sect as "Gnostic."[18] It is becoming increasingly clear that the knowledge of the Qumran texts is of a more practical, less speculative kind, than that of second-century Gnosticism. The function of knowledge, as seen in these texts, is to bring the possessor into right moral and religious relationship to God. To be sure, there are intellectual aspects. The initiates understand the purposes of God with respect to the end time. They are thus led to bring their lives into conformity with the divine will. But the thought as a whole is closer to Daniel than to the Gnostic systems of the second century and following. In Daniel "the wise," those who understand God's eschatological purpose now being worked out in the world, devote themselves to righteousness (obedience to the law), as befits "the saints of the Most High," the possessors of the coming kingdom. At Qumran the wise likewise dedicate themselves to the law, as interpreted by the Teacher of Righteousness and others, that they may be prepared to receive the sovereignty over the world soon to be given them by God. The knowledge referred to, then, in the Qumran texts is of the kind proper to apocalyptic eschatology.

Understanding of the purpose and plans of God with respect to the end time and of the divine requirements for admission to the coming kingdom is precisely what one finds in the Gospel of Matthew. W. D. Davies some time ago saw the basic similarity between the kind of knowledge spoken of in Matt. 11: 25-30 and in the Qumran texts.[19] But he did not see how deeply this eschatological knowledge affects the theology of the Gospel

[18] See the article by W. D. Davies referred to in note 9; also Friedrich Nötscher, *Zur theologischen Terminologie der Qumran-Texte* (Bonn, 1956), pp. 15 ff., and Hans Joachim Schoeps, *Ugmeinde, Judenchristentum, Gnosis* (Tübingen, 1956).

[19] *Op. cit.*

as a whole. God makes known to the disciples what Jesus himself knows: who he is, what his work in the world is, and what he will do at the last. The disciples are led to understand that faith in him and obedience to the law as interpreted by and exemplified in him will lead to the higher righteousness, possession of which will result in admission to the kingdom of heaven.

The fourth characteristic of Matthew's Christology concerns the prominence of the Son of Man concept and its fusion with the Son of God ideology. What can be said about the historical relations of this combination?

It is significant that among Stephen's last words appears a reference to Jesus as "the Son of Man" (Acts 7:56). This term is rarely found on the lips of anyone but Jesus himself. From this fact Cullmann concludes that the Son of Man Christology may have had its home among the Hellenists.[20] However that may be, Stephen uses the term, and apparently to indicate Jesus' role as coming Judge. This heavenly Son of Man is to destroy the temple and change the traditional customs, obviously at his return, and there may be significance in the fact that he is said to be *standing* at the right hand of God (7:55). This may suggest that even now he is ready for his glorious return. The fact that Stephen addresses prayer to the "Lord Jesus" (7:59) is worth noticing, although it is difficult to know what to make of it. F. F. Bruce thinks it "an early, if tacit, testimony to the Christian belief in our Lord's essential deity." [21] However, Simon is surely right in urging caution here, for it may mean no more than a request for Jesus "to usher him [Stephen] into the presence of the Almighty." [22] The data are

[20] *Die Christologie des Neuen Testaments*, pp. 167 ff.
[21] *Commentary on the Book of Acts* (Grand Rapids: Wm. B. Eerdmans Publishing Co., 1954), p. 171.
[22] *Op. cit.*, p. 66.

not at hand in Stephen's address for saying positively that his Christology joins the Son of Man and the Son of God categories. But such a deduction is not excluded.

No parallel can be drawn with the Qumran texts for the simple reason that the terms Son of Man and Son of God as messianic designations do not appear in the material thus far discovered. Though fragments of portions of I Enoch have been found at Qumran, none representing the similitudes (Chs. 37-71)—the section in which the description of the Son of Man is contained—has been discovered.[23] One passage in The Rule of the Congregation seems to refer to God's begetting of the Messiah, perhaps an allusion to Ps. 2: 7. If this reading of the text is correct,[24] the Messiah is thought of as in some sense the Son of God, even though the term is not used.

Perhaps the closest parallel to the confluence of the Son of Man and the Son of God categories in the Christology of Matthew is to be found in the Fourth Gospel. It will be remembered that it was said in Chapter II that in Matt. 14: 33 we come closer to the Hellenistic Son of God concept (a divine being who accredits himself as such by charismatic phenomena) than anywhere else in the Synoptic Gospels and that in other passages of Matthew Jesus is clearly conceived as belonging to the world of deity. Lohmeyer's judgment that the Christology of Matt. 28: 18-20 is as exalted as that reached in the Fourth Gospel may be cited again.

We may agree with C. H. Dodd that the statements made about the Son of Man in the Fourth Gospel recall the figure of the heavenly Anthropos as it appears in Hellenistic documents and speculative Judaism: the Being "who is the arche-

[23] J. T. Milik, *op. cit.*, p. 33.

[24] On the problem see Robert Gordis, "The 'Begotten' Messiah in the Qumran Scrolls," *Vetus Testamentum*, VII (1957), 191-94; Morton Smith, " 'God's Begetting the Messiah' in 1QSa," *New Testament Studies*, V (1958/59), 218-24.

type of the human race, and at the same time the true or essential humanity resident or immanent in individuals of the human species; who is the offspring of the Supreme God and destined to be reunited with Him." [25] This Son of Man or Son of God descended from heaven and ascended again to heaven, gathering up into himself those who believe in him and live according to his commandments. Now the Christology of Matthew does not explicate so clearly the Son of Man mythology as does the Fourth Gospel, but there can be little doubt that the thought is moving in the same general direction. The Jesus of Matthew is "God with us" to bring believers into the kingdom of heaven. We have clearly in Matthew no "exaltation" Christology.

Cullmann has argued strongly that the Fourth Gospel is fundamentally related to the circle represented by the Hellenists and the Qumran community. Is it possible that the Gospel of Matthew may be somehow related to this same circle of thought and that certain contacts between the First and the Fourth Gospels may thus be explained? [26]

[25] *The Interpretation of the Fourth Gospel* (Cambridge: The University Press, 1953), p. 244.

[26] It is impossible to comment here in detail on the striking similarities between several features of the First and the Fourth Gospels. We have noted the decided liking of both writers for the term "Father" on the lips of Jesus, the confluence and dominance of the Son of Man and Son of God categories in each Gospel, the use of the second Moses ideology in both. P. Nepper-Christensen (*Das Matthäusevangelium* [Aarhus, 1958], Ch. V) has noted the strong and similar interest in the fulfillment of Old Testament prophecy, even to the formulas of citation. N. A. Dahl ("Die Passionsgeschichte bei Matthäus," *New Testament Studies,* II [1955/56], 21, 32) and his student Peder Borgen ("John and the Synoptics in the Passion Narrative," *New Testament Studies,* V [1958/59], 246-59) have pointed out many striking similarities in the two Passion narratives. These scholars hold that the relationship cannot be explained by assuming direct use of Matthew by the Fourth Evangelist but by influence of the Synoptic tradition on the tradition behind the Fourth Gospel. Further research is needed in order to account adequately for the peculiar relationship of these two Gospels.

How might the relationships be conceived? We learn from the book of Acts that it was the Hellenists who, after being driven out of Jerusalem, undertook a mission to Gentiles in the city of Antioch (11:20). It has been thought likely by many scholars that the Gospel of Matthew was written in Syria, perhaps in Antioch or the hinterland of this city. Is the Gospel of Matthew the sort of a revision of the Gospel of Mark that one of these Hellenists (or a disciple) would make, while the Fourth Gospel represents the tradition of the Hellenists in purer form, unconditioned and unfettered by the point of view on the career of Jesus represented in Mark and Q? The similarities we have noted between the Gospel of Matthew on the one side and the Hellenists, the sectarians of Qumran, and the Fourth Gospel on the other lie in Matthew's peculiar materials and the editorial element introduced by him. Was he consciously preserving and interpreting traditions different from his own for a church which found itself the heir of unreconciled traditions? His role, then, would not be unlike that played by the Deuteronomic or Priestly editors of the Old Testament.

If Matthew's peculiar materials and the general point of view he represents root in the views of this Jewish-Christian "Hellenist" group of Jerusalem, a number of data receive an explanation. Let us attempt to summarize some of them (including points already mentioned):

1) The Jewish outlook of the Gospel, almost universally noted, is adequately accounted for: the strong interest in the fulfillment of the prophecies of the Old Testament; the high regard for the law of Moses in its true interpretation; the lack of explanation of elements of Jewish piety; the apocalyptic eschatology; the avoidance of the divine name in the phrase "the kingdom of heaven"; Semitic words and idioms; the limitation of the mission of Jesus to Israel (see further below); and the Jewish qualities of mind exhibited in the love of stereotyping, repetition, schematizing, and the like. Bacon's judgment

that the author was "a scribe who has been trained for the kingdom of heaven" (Matt. 13:52) can still be maintained, only he will be seen not as having belonged to the school of the Pharisaic rabbi Johanan ben Zakkai but rather to sectarian Judaism as represented by the Hellenists and perhaps by the men of Qumran.

2) The presence of elements of primitive Jerusalem tradition in Matthew's reworking of the Marcan passion story (such as the story concerning the end of Judas—Matt. 27:3-10), pointed out by Dahl, Stendahl, and Kilpatrick, receive an adequate explanation. The Hellenists obviously carried with them to Syria a cycle of materials partly similar to and different from other lines of tradition. Perhaps this material is in part represented by the materials assigned by Streeter to M (the teaching material peculiar to Matthew) and also by the some dozen edifying stories (e.g., Peter's walking on the water, the temple tax episode, and the several Matthean additions to the Passion and Resurrection narratives). It will be recalled that Streeter believed that M came from Jerusalem to Antioch.

3) The universalistic note in Matthew is adequately accounted for. There is a strange duality in the reference to the work of the Hellenists in Acts 11:19-20: they spoke the word "to none except Jews"; but some of them "spoke to the Greeks also." [27] Since the Hellenists were Jews, they naturally were persuaded of Israel's unique role in the purposes of God and undoubtedly saw Jesus' mission as directed to the Jewish people, as indeed it historically was.[28] The basic purpose of the Hellenists, as we saw, was to rid Israel of distortions of the Mosaic law (including the temple and its sacrificial worship)

[27] Whether the original reading here was Ἕλληνας or Ἑλληνιστάς the reference is to Gentiles, as the contrast with Ἰουδαῖοι of v. 19 shows (Lake and Cadbury in F. J. Foakes Jackson and K. Lake [eds.], *The Beginnings of Christianity* [London: Macmillan & Co., Ltd., 1920-33], IV, 128).

[28] Joachim Jeremias, *Jesus' Promise to the Nations, passim.*

and to bring about in Israel acceptance of Jesus as the second Moses. In their own eyes the Hellenists were intensely loyal to Judaism. But official Judaism did not so regard them. They were repudiated as heretics and renegades and driven out of Jerusalem. Though they loved Israel and felt that their mission was to the Chosen People, they saw that they could no longer carry out the mission, at least not at the national center of Judaism. They could work at best on the fringes, in Samaria (where their hostility to the Jerusalem temple would find sympathetic support and where belief in the coming of a second Moses was strong) and among the Jews of the Diaspora. Their own rejection at the hands of official Judaism led them to ponder deeply on the purposes of God and to conclude that his judgment would speedily fall on the nation, that the kingdom of God would be taken away from the Jews and "given to a nation producing the fruits of it" (Matt. 21:43). Thus, the sheer logic of the events through which they had passed impelled some of them into a Gentile mission, though many of them continued to work among Diaspora Jews. The antipathy toward official Judaism, the love of true Judaism (as explicated by Jesus, the second Moses), and the universalism expressed in the Gospel of Matthew all are understandable if the author belonged to the circle of the Hellenists from Jerusalem and their disciples.

4) The ready acceptance of the Gospel of Matthew in the Gentile churches, on the one hand, and among the Ebionites, on the other, is explained. Poul Nepper-Christensen rightly points out that if this Gospel was written for Jewish-Christian readers it is hard to explain how it became popular so quickly in the Gentile churches.[29] But if the author was a Hellenist of the type known from Acts, with the broad outlook we have attributed to him, and who edited traditions other than his own

[29] *Op. cit.*, p. 206.

in a way intelligible to Gentile readers, the speedy acceptance of this Gospel is not strange.

The high reverence in which the apostle Matthew was held by the Ebionites, the Jewish-Christian sectarians of Transjordan of early Christian centuries, is apparent from special mention of him in the first of the fragments of the Ebionite Gospel preserved in Epiphanius.[30] It is possible that the Ebionites wished to suggest that the Gospel used by them was written by Matthew. The assertion of certain church fathers that the Ebionites used a mutilated and perverted Gospel of Matthew cannot be positively validated, but it appears probable.

If the background we have suggested for the author of the Gospel of Matthew is correct, the attractiveness of this Gospel for the Ebionites is explained in part. We have found affinities between the thought of the Gospel of Matthew and the views of both the Hellenists and the Qumran sectarians. Strong similarities seem to exist between the theology of the Qumran texts and that of the Ebionites.[31] It is possible that at least some of the sectarians of Qumran merged with the Ebionites after the destruction of Qumran by the Romans about A.D. 68.[32] Though parts of the Gospel of Matthew would be unacceptable to the Ebionites (they rejected the Virgin Birth, for example, and explained Jesus' sonship as the result of the coming of the Spirit on him at the baptism), they would find the Jewish elements of this Gospel and the emphasis on the special knowledge possessed by the Elect especially congenial. Matthew's story about the temple tax would appeal to them, for, like the Hellenists and

[30] See E. Hennecke and W. Schneemelcher, *Neutestamentliche Apokryphen* (3. *Aufl.;* Tübingen, 1959), I, 100 ff.

[31] Hans Joachim Schoeps, *Urgemeinde, Judenchristentum, Gnosis, passim.*

[32] Oscar Cullmann in K. Galling (ed.), *Die Religion in Geschichte und Gegenwart* (3. *Aufl.;* Tübingen, 1957—), II, 298.

to a degree the sectarians of Qumran, they opposed the temple cultus.

Other advantages of the thought background of the Gospel of Matthew tentatively suggested might be pointed out if space permitted, but we must look in conclusion at the relevance of Matthew's Christology for the situation of the church at the time when the Gospel appeared.

It seems apparent from the use of Mark by Matthew, the rather obvious allusion to the fall of Jerusalem in Matthew's form of the parable of the Great Feast (Matt. 22:7), and the general conditions in the church indirectly suggested, that the Gospel of Matthew must be dated in the last quarter of the first century. What these conditions were may be briefly indicated.

First, it is obvious that the church was locked in bitter struggle with the synagogue. Judaism had set itself firmly against Christianity. Kilpatrick, who cites in detail the evidence for this,[33] quotes a benediction of Samuel the Small at Jamnia in the time of Gamaliel II (*ca.* A.D. 85) which condemns the Christians so strongly that it is clear that attendance at the synagogue was no longer possible for them: "For the excommunicate let there be no hope and the arrogant government do thou swiftly uproot in our days; and may the Christians and the heretics suddenly be laid low and not be inscribed with the righteous. Blessed art thou, O Lord, who humblest the arrogant."[34] Christian writings were beginning to be condemned and sought out for destruction. Active attempts to counter Christian teachings were launched. Social intercourse was stopped and outbreaks of actual persecution occurred. The intensity of the hostility between the two groups is to be seen in the book of Revelation (*ca.* A.D. 95), where the writer bit-

[33] *The Origins of the Gospel According to St. Matthew* (Oxford: Clarendon Press, 1946), Ch. VI.

[34] *Ibid.*, p. 109.

terly labels the persecutors of the church the "synagogue of Satan" (2:9; 3:9). A like hostility is to be seen in the Fourth Gospel (*ca.* A.D. 95-115) where "the Jews" are lumped together into one undifferentiated category and unsparingly condemned.

The church needed a writing which would clearly define the relationship of Christianity to Judaism and offer a rationale for its existence. Were the Jews or the Christians the people of God, the heirs of the coming kingdom? On whom would the judgment of God fall, on the Jews or on the Christians? The author of Matthew presented an apologetic for the church partly by appealing to Jesus himself, who had supplied in his own controversies with the Jews the needed answers.

The Jesus of Matthew presents himself as the fulfiller of the law and the prophets. He fulfilled them in that he obeyed their true requirements by acting in the spirit of love and mercy; and he showed his disciples what they really require of men. He fulfilled them by effecting the redemption to which they point. He brought about forgiveness of sins for men. He opposed the blind religious leaders who elevated unimportant elements of the law to a primary place and who were concerned about external rather than internal righteousness. The Jesus of the Gospel of Matthew seems to say, "If you follow me, you are following Moses as he ought to be followed. My disciples and I are the true Jews."

The genealogy and the nativity stories obviously are intended to counter the Jewish attack on Jesus' right to be regarded as the Messiah. The genealogy claims that he was indeed by legal right the Son of David and the nativity stories show that he was not an illegitimate child but the very Son of God. At the baptism and at the transfiguration God himself declared Jesus to be his only Son, an answer to the Jewish objection that God had no "Son." Jesus' great deeds of power show him to be the second Moses and the true Son of God. His death was no evidence that he was an imposter, for he rose from the grave victorious over death and his enemies. That he really rose and was not spirited away by his disciples is evident from the fact that the tomb was guarded (Matt. 27:62-66; 28:11-15). Cosmic disturbances attended his death (Matt. 27:51 ff.). His appearance on a mountain in Galilee invested with "all authority in heaven and on earth" (Matt. 28:16-20) presages his return in glory as Judge of the world. Those who accept and follow him will inherit the coming kingdom, but those who reject him will be cast out into the outer darkness. The book as a whole is a glowing apologetic for the church in its controversy with Judaism.

Second, the church was attempting to win all men to faith in Jesus as God's way of salvation. To accomplish this goal it was necessary to portray Jesus in ways that could be understood not only by Jews but by Gentiles also. We have seen how Matthew's portrait would appeal to Jews. But what features of it would speak effectively to Gentiles?

The presentation of Jesus as the Son of God—as a divine-human being who had been born of a virgin, who had validated his supernatural origin by his miraculous powers, whose true identity and function had been revealed to men by the Father so that they might understand and be saved—is superbly designed to speak to the mind of the time.

Kings and emperors had long been hailed as sons of God and divine saviors. Particularly in the East the Roman Caesar played the role of the divine savior so common in the syncretistic religions of the time. Dositheus, the teacher of Simon Magus, gave himself out as "the Son of God" and Simon after him was hailed as "that power of God which is called Great" (Acts 8:10).[35] The latter is regarded by several church fathers as the first Gnostic. His disciples carried his teachings to Antioch, to Alexandria, and elsewhere. Many prophets, some

[35] On Simon Magus see Robert M. Grant, *Gnosticism and Early Christianity* (New York: Columbia University Press, 1959), Ch. III.

regarding themselves as pre-existent beings, offered themselves as objects of faith and promised deliverance to their followers. A "Son of God" as a divine savior come to earth for the redemption of men was a common idea in the syncretistic religions of the period.[36] The Elect were regarded as possessing knowledge concerning this savior and the way of deliverance. In a period when revealed knowledge was being so much stressed, as is evident from the Qumran texts, other Jewish apocalyptic writings (such as I Enoch), the New Testament (especially Paul and the Fourth Evangelist), the letters of Ignatius of Antioch, other writings of the Fathers, and the new Nag-Hammadi manuscripts,[37] it would be strange if religious writings of a propagandist nature (such as our Gospels are in part) did not utilize the current terminology and ideology for their own ends.

It is significant, therefore, that in the Gospel of Matthew the true identity and function of Jesus is revealed to the Elect and that these are said to "understand" the saving revelation. Such a concept would have been understood by Jews and Gentiles alike in the time of the writing of the Gospel of Matthew.

Finally, Matthew's portrait of Jesus is so drawn as to challenge Christians to moral and spiritual growth and thus to preparedness for the coming of the kingdom of heaven. The letters to the seven churches contained in the book of Revelation indicate clearly that false teachers were at work subverting the morals of Christians. The Pastoral Epistles likewise disclose the pernicious teachings being propagated by purveyors of false knowledge. "They profess to know God, but they deny

[36] See Benjamin Wisner Bacon, *The Gospel of the Hellenists* (New York: Henry Holt & Co., 1933), Ch. XI; Rudolf Bultmann, *Theology of the New Testament* (New York: Charles Scribner's Sons, 1951-55), I, 164 ff.

[37] See Robert M. Grant, *op. cit., passim.*

him by their deeds" (Titus 1:16). Jews who left the synagogue for the freer atmosphere of the church often were tempted to swing over to a life of unbridled freedom and Gentiles who came into the church out of heathenism tended to carry their pagan ways with them. How were such to be made into loyal disciples of Jesus and to be prepared for the coming judgment and the kingdom of heaven?

We read much in Matthew about "false prophets," "evildoers" (7:15 ff.), who are likened to tares growing among the wheat (13:36 ff.) or to a man without a wedding garment (22:11-13). The true Christian for our author is not only one who shares in the knowledge that Jesus is the Christ, the Son of the living God, but one who obeys the words of Jesus (7:21 ff.; 11:29; 28:20) and who imitates him in sacrificial, loving service (16:24 ff.; 25:31 ff.). When one imitates and obeys Jesus, he is obeying the law of Moses as it was meant to be obeyed. Such a man possesses the higher righteousness; he is inwardly, not simply externally, good. Those who are like Jesus will enter the kingdom of heaven; all others will be cast into the furnace of fire, when the Son of Man comes to judge the world.

Matthew's Jesus is a commanding figure. He is painted on a cosmic canvas with the pigments which many writers and cultures had emptied into his paintpot. He appears at the end of the Gospel on a mountain, like Yahweh of old, giving commandments to his people and promising to be with them in their earthly journeyings. To the faithful he will say at the last, "Come, O blessed of my Father, inherit the kingdom prepared for you from the foundation of the world" (25:34).

INDEX OF PASSAGES

Old Testament

New Testament

Apocrypha, Pseudepigrapha, and Other Jewish Literature

Rabbinic Writings

The Fathers

INDEX OF PERSONS AND SUBJECTS